D0401934

CYBER GOLD RUSH!

Turning knowledge into gold

Dr Alan Cook & Heather Duggan

Mountain, Brisbane, Australia

Readers should not interpret mention of companies or products in this book as endorsements. Nor should they interpret mention of companies as recommendations to invest in those companies. If we have inadvertently used any copyrighted material or trademarks please inform us and corrections will be made in future editions. Alan Cook & Heather Duggan

© 2000 Alan Cook & Heather Duggan

All rights reserved, including the right of reproduction in whole or in part in any form by any means.

Composition: David Wrigley, Avid Desktop Design, Brisbane, Queensland.
Printed and bound in Australia by Merino Litho, Brisbane, Queensland.

Cyber Gold Rush!: Turning Knowledge into Gold / by Dr. Alan Cook and Heather Duggan.
1. Investment. 2. Technology. 3. Business. 4. Future trends. 5. Current affairs. 6. Jobs.

Published by
Mountain Pty Ltd
PO Box 556
New Farm, Queensland, 4005
Australia.

ISBN 0-646-33462-X

Contents

CYBER GOLD RUSH!

The Cyber Gold Rush

Future Trends in Technology, Business, Science & Society

Introduction

We have called this time in our lives 'The Cyber Gold Rush' because the most obvious trend that is occurring in the developed world involves the headlong rush by entrepreneurs to exploit opportunities provided by commerce on the Internet. Computers have changed the way we work. The Internet has changed the way we communicate. Electronic commerce is beginning to take off and that will be eclipsed by business-to-business transactions. Even large companies realise that they are not big enough to compete on the global stage so mergers, alliances and joint ventures between companies have proliferated. We are living in a time of great social, economic and environmental upheaval. There is an unprecedented range of opportunities for the growth of industry, the economy and hence changes to our lifestyle. Change is taking place, at the same time, on many different fronts.

Science and Technology promise fundamental changes to the way we live. The field of human genetics promises cures for debilitating inherited diseases but also presents us with difficult ethical dilemmas. Genetic manipulation of crops is considered foolhardy by some and by others, a remedy for third world poverty and famine. Smarter devices that offer a wide variety of functions will replace the electronic goods we now use. Big businesses have discovered that there is money to be made in mass education and we can expect the information age to change the way we teach and learn. Miscreants have discovered that modern technology provides opportunities for big profits from criminal activity. The baby boomer generation are unlikely to retire quietly and will have a significant influence on society. Governments will have to make difficult decisions about tax collection, the environment and new technology.

This book sets out to capture the excitement of these times by identifying some of the major changes occurring at this moment as described in the media and on the Internet. We hope it helps you better understand the world in the midst of the cyber gold rush.

Alan Cook & Heather Duggan

Part One:

Business

CYBER GOLD RUSH!

☆ Main Point

Dropouts from business schools and some of the biggest tycoons in the world are working at a frenzied pace to ensure that they can take advantage of opportunities presented by telecommunications and the Internet.

✓ Executive Summary

Bright young entrepreneurs with plenty of nerve have discovered that becoming part of the surge in telecommunications and Internet development can be a heady and, for some, a profitable experience. Never before have people with good ideas and little capital been able to bring their ideas to fruition so fast. This is partly because backers realise that the cyber gold rush is a unique period in history that will see new ways of doing business, communicating and delivering entertainment. They also realise that there is considerable advantage in being first with an idea. And they realise that size is not important - minnows can make a significant contribution.

> **"** Windows this large don't open often. **"**

Often much slower at the start, big business, has also discovered the potential of these technological advances. Benefiting from sizeable cash flow and brand names they have begun to compete by entering into joint ventures with established players or taking up shares in front runners. This has been particularly the case for media companies. Seeing both the threat of competition from the Internet and the potential it represents, they have moved to include an Internet presence in their portfolio. Indeed the potential synergies that can be exploited between TV, the Internet, telecommunications, the entertainment industry, the print media, news agencies and sport are some of the most exciting business prospects today.

> **"** Those who have succeeded in the on-line world are invariably young, focused and totally committed to the task. **"**

❖ The Big Ideas

☐ Upstarts and Start-Ups

Young people with bright business ideas have dropped out of US business schools over the past year and flocked to Silicon Valley venture capitalists looking for money to bring an idea to the stage when a company can be floated on the stock exchange. It is still tough going but having connections can expedite the search for money. Many give up after their idea has been rejected for the n'th time. But the lucky few will have found someone who is prepared to invest in their ideas. Being the first with an idea helps. More US venture capital was invested in businesses last year than ever before. Most of the businesses supported by venture capitalists will never make a profit. A few will become very big.

At the same time, recent graduates, wanting 'a piece of the action' queue, at recruitment fairs, to give their resumes to companies that might not offer a big salary but instead a chance to make a fortune from share options. More established companies that merely offer a reasonable salary and security may not appeal as much to a young person with a good degree, mountains of energy and the willingness to rough it for a year or so until the money comes pouring in. New recruits are often 'thrown into the deep end' and expected to participate in the frenzied activity that is necessary to bring an initial idea to the stage when the company can be floated, the initial public offering, the IPO.

❒ Venture Capital (VC) Funds in Australia

While money spent by venture capitalists in the US has reached unprecedented heights it has still been tight in Australia, especially for people with bright ideas who need seed money. This is where a new investment group, TiNSHED, comes in. They plan to support small Australian companies as well as promising ideas from overseas. However, prospective businesses would need to have a strong management team and their business plan will have to go through a rigorous examination before it is supported.

❒ Initial Public Offering (IPO)

Once a business has some backing it can implement its plan which often results in a float of shares on the stock market, an initial public offering. With so much interest in exploiting opportunities in telecommunications and the Internet, a spate of IPOs has hit the markets both in Australia and overseas. Nearly forty IPOs were floated in Australia in the month before Christmas 99 and several more came just after the New

Year. A large percentage of these businesses were in the technology and Internet sectors.

Many of the entrepreneurs who are developing these businesses are in their late twenties or early thirties. Typically they have training and experience in business, technology or commerce, they have a bright idea and see a 'once in a lifetime opportunity' to build a business and make a lot of money. At this stage in their lives they are prepared to work frenetically and use their life savings or borrow heavily, simply because the potential rewards are so great. If success comes, it is not only through an obsessive dedication to a goal, but also a business plan that finds a specific focus rather than a broad one. The Australian company, Sinewave Interactive, for instance, specialises in two areas: a technique that helps a site ensure that it is placed high in search engine lists; and the Top 100 web site that lists the most popular sites. The company, Active Concepts, has produced software that lets companies determine how many sales result from hits on a web site. Telemedia Networks International develops call-centre software and databases for voicemail systems. These niche products have brought great rewards to their inventors. Success also depends on others seeing the worth of the product then using it, licensing it or, in some cases, buying the company. Yahoo, for instance, has bought twelve other companies over the past two years.

" Some big companies may have been slow to discover the net but they can catch up because of their size and customer loyalty. "

☐ Big Business Interests

It is not only young upstarts who have now seen the potential of the Internet and the deregulation of telecommunications. Microsoft, for instance, has used its fabulous wealth to establish a presence in the travel, car and banking industries. A leading travel agency, seeing the danger of competition from on-line travel agents and direct selling by airlines, reinvented itself as a fulfilment agency for on-line sales. Banks and financial institutions started on-line share trading. It took the stockbroking industry some time to react. Eventually realising the threat, many of the biggest brokers worldwide have now embraced the Internet. Music and book store chains have recognised the threat that on-line stores like Amazon and CDNow represent and have developed a net presence. Many of these dot.com adjuncts have yet to show a profit but businesses believe it is important, if only for the purposes of visibility, to have a web site.

" The Internet presents a totally different way of doing business. "

In Australia, some of the biggest investors in telecommunications and the Internet are Telstra, the Packer family through PBL and the Murdoch family through News Corporation. Smaller companies such as Computershare, Solution 6, Sausage Software and One.Tel have all benefited from the backing of one or more of these big three. Seeing the threat of the Internet and Pay TV to their existing sources of income from television and magazines, PBL has invested wisely in these two growing areas. In just over a year they have seen their investment of $25 million in the Internet site ninemsn (a joint venture with Microsoft) grow to be valued at $250 million.

Meanwhile, in a frenzy of deal making, in November 1999, News Corporation, with fifteen or so other deals on the table, bought a 10.8% share of the Internet health care company, Healtheon. The deal means that Healtheon products will be more widely advertised on News Corp outlets and News Corporation can include health content in its TV, radio, book and newspaper outlets. Lastly, News Corporation has also formed a partnership with Softbank to act as a venture capitalist for Internet companies.

Softbank, run by Masayoshi Son is, perhaps, the biggest investor in the Internet worldwide. It has invested US$1.7 billion dollars in over one hundred Internet companies. The approach has been to identify a wide variety of companies that offer massive 'eyeball traffic'. An offshoot, Softbank Technology Ventures has provided seed money for start-ups with potential, then poured more money into those that prove to have the greatest prospects. Some companies did not succeed because the technology required was not yet commonplace. Other start-ups folded because their product demanded a greater change in behaviour than the general public were prepared to commit to. Nevertheless, the investment success rate for Softbank has been phenomenal.

THE INTERNET REVOLUTION

☆ Main Point

E-commerce and business-to-business transactions will dominate Internet developments over the next few years. Although many businesses will benefit from this expansion, companies that control the portals to the Internet are likely to benefit the most. These companies will already be big, will already have an Internet presence and already serve a large number of customers.

✓ Executive Summary

The big winners in the e-commerce revolution will be those who control the portals. Developing a successful portal will be an expensive enterprise. These organisations will already be established in the Internet world, will have access to large databases of customers and have already in place (or are fast completing) alliances with other large organisations in the media, in telecommunications, distribution, banking or retailing.

" We can be sure of two things. The Internet revolution presents us with wonderful opportunities and even greater uncertainties. **"**

However, which companies emerge as the dominant forces in the race for Internet market share depends on companies making the correct moves in the next few years (or rapidly correcting mistakes). There will be little room for error and yet, because the playing field is replete with uncertainties, wrong moves are very likely for most players.

Vendors who prosper in an e-commerce world will be those who plan everything with customer satisfaction in mind. Customers will demand good service and shift allegiance to another vendor if they are dissatisfied. This means that the simplicity of a site, interactions between the customer and the vendor, efficiency of service completion and attention to customer satisfaction will need special attention if customer loyalty is to be retained.

" We used to worry about 'bums on seats'. Now all that matters is 'eyeballs on sites.' That's why portals should be very profitable. **"**

❖ The Big Ideas

❑ Advantages of Electronic Commerce

Choosing to use the Internet for business is easy for some companies. For instance, because music can be digitised, there is no need for a supplier to mail a CD to a customer. Companies will now send to you, over the Internet, the digitised music from an entire CD, just one track or a compilation of tracks, specially requested by you, from a number of CDs. You can then down-load the music at home. Videotapes, books, magazines, professional journals, and software are also capable of digital rather than physical transmission to customers.

General Motors predicts that the increased efficiencies that will come about by using e-commerce for purchase of parts, and raw materials and sale of vehicles will save it A$18 billion. They will also be able to build a car 'to order' for a customer. So, other benefits of e-commerce are improvement of customer service, increase of exchange of information with a customer and increased customer loyalty. By the year 2003 an IBM representative predicted that electronic commerce would represent 10% of financial transactions worldwide.

❝ We are in the midst of a revolution during which companies ignore e-commerce at their peril. **❞**

❑ Selling on the Internet

E-business is not the same as normal business. New thinking is required. New sales strategies, new relationships with suppliers and customers and new ways of conducting transactions are needed. Because trust is a key element in retaining customer loyalty, businesses need to develop seamless and timely communications with customers and efficient distribution and 'return-for-refund' systems.

Some items are more easily sold on the Internet than others are. People are more likely to buy books, music and travel and tickets to concerts (items that are well defined and where quality is predictable). Items that require touching such as clothes and sports equipment are also bought in reasonable volume - perhaps because the provider guaranteed quality or return, free of charge, for a refund. Insurance companies, who sell their products through brokers, find it difficult to sell on-line, partly because it is difficult for the general public to choose between competing policies without advice from a broker.

Companies that start on-line businesses need to be aware that setting up an efficient business on-line is not cheap. For instance they need to factor in the cost of warehousing and distribution. These can be as much as 15% of sales. If you are selling physical goods, responding to customer e-mail and telephone inquiries, fulfilling orders, processing credit card charges, shipping goods and ordering raw materials from suppliers make up the bulk of a surprisingly labour-intensive industry.

" By 1998 more Australian International business was done over the net than was done over the phone. **"**

Companies selling on-line are spending millions of dollars on conventional advertising (TV, radio, newspapers, billboards) trying to attract customers to their sites. The jury is still out on the most effective ways of attracting visitors. One popular means of exposing your site is to pay for banner advertising on a portal that has a heavy throughput of customers. This, too, can be quite expensive and its effectiveness is still being debated. Other issues to consider include the need for competitive pricing, keeping enough inventory to satisfy peak demand quickly, keeping customers satisfied and selling in a 24 hour a day-7 day a week, on-line world.

" We are in an excellent position to be a leading e-commerce nation in this part of the world. **"**

Web sites need to be user-friendly to be successful. This means that simplicity (an absence of ambiguity), usefulness (interactivity) and attractiveness should be key attributes. Those sites will prosper that, although catering to a mass market, make customers feel that they are receiving personal service. For instance, a customer who has sent a book order to Amazon.com is likely to receive e-mail from Amazon suggesting other books in the same category.

It has been predicted that Internet sales will increase by 50% a year over the next three years. By the year 2003 Internet sales will explode as Generation Y (15-24 year olds) start to earn money.

☐ Emerging Strategies

The philosophy of some Web-site owners is that, if you can convince enough people to look at your site, you will be able to charge others to advertise on it. The problem, however, is that there does not seem to be a direct connection between the number of hits a site receives and the number of orders an advertiser at the site receives. So advertisers are beginning to request more sophisticated measures of site effectiveness. These might take into consideration the number of unique visitors and the length of a visit to the site by a potential customer.

There are those who have decided that cooperation is a better Internet strategy than competition. One vendor, faced with worldwide competition from rival Internet-based companies decided that, rather than compete with them, he would set up a portal where customers could view not only his products but related and even competing products from other companies. In other words, instead of competing for market share, he would endeavour to expand the market.

Before too long we will see differentiated pricing structures for customers similar to 'priority paid' postal services. This will provide urgent communications, such as key orders, to be sent and processed rapidly, but at a premium price.

❏ From a Purchaser Viewpoint

❝ It is better to work with others to make a bigger e-commerce pie than it is to compete with them for a smaller pie. ❞

People are likely to choose to shop on the Internet because it saves time, they can buy things more cheaply, they can comparison shop, do not have to wait in queues or deal with salespeople and, in some cases, can avoid paying tax. They will also buy using the Internet if a service is convenient. The question remains whether customers will shop for supermarket items on-line. Well-organised customers might e-mail their shopping list to a supplier for later delivery to their home. For the rest of us less organised souls a regular but brief homeward detour to a local store or take-away (an activity euphemistically labelled 'two-bag shopping') might continue to be more popular than a weekly shopping expedition.

The Internet will present many advantages for the busy shopper. Let us say that you want to buy a digital camera with features A, B and C and you want to pay no more than $400. You will be able to put a request in the hands of an Internet search company that will use software (shop bots) to not only find the best deal but organise payment for, and delivery of, the item.

The Australian Bureau of Statistics reported that three million purchases were made on the Internet in Australia in 1998 (an increase of nearly 60% over the previous year). Books, magazines, software and computers were the most common purchases. In 1999 about 2% of Australians bought on-line.

By 2005 a quarter of consumer spending (in developed nations) will be over the Internet.

☐ Building Web Sites & Maintaining Market Share in a Global Economy

Conventional wisdom is that, for many companies, quickly developing a presence on the Internet is vital if they are to maintain market share. In the US, rather than building a site from scratch, companies are making use of proprietary web design software. This notwithstanding, the speed with which companies and individuals are forcing themselves into this mad scramble for share of the market is taking its toll. Reports indicate that, in such places as Silicon Valley, the business of psychiatrists and psychologists treating stress has never been brisker.

The Internet provides vastly increased communication between businesses worldwide. This is an opportunity for companies with good products and an aggressive sales policy to expand into new markets. It is also a threat to those who hitherto served an essentially closed, home market with mediocre product and service. Australian companies need to beware of overseas companies, especially US companies, pushing into their markets. The best way to defend against this is to establish a local presence and build and retain a loyal client base. Language is still a barrier to world e-commerce and software that can translate from one language to another in real time has to be the 'killer application' that will finally break open world business.

Alliances, joint ventures and mergers have been a common feature of business development over the past year as computer companies, and those in media and telecommunications, seek synergies with complementary businesses in order to exploit e-business opportunities in a rapidly evolving but uncertain environment. We are likely to see small and medium sized businesses also do this as they see the benefits of economies of scale, increased buying power and the advantages of out-sourcing non-core business.

☐ Portals run by 'Commerce Service Providers'

The Internet portal is likely to become the cash cow of the Internet. Companies like ecorp and Telstra, both with substantial

" Getting first to market is a huge challenge but promises fabulous rewards. **"**

" Keeping just a neck ahead of the competition in this cyber race is pressure beyond belief. **"**

> **"** Free e-mail has become a good carrot to increase visitor numbers for a portal. **"**

cash backing, an established Internet presence and an aggressive expansion policy, stand to be able to benefit from an explosion in e-commerce. Both already have a large, daily, customer flow-through and are rapidly signing up businesses to advertise and conduct transactions through their portal. The key to their attractiveness to business is their large customer database, but they are likely to provide many more services to vendors such as credit checks, payment processing, distribution and returns.

The requirements for entry into the elite club of portal owners (a large customer base, extensive cash backing, established Internet presence) means that large companies that have already entered the game are likely to dominate the field. These may stand alone or form partnerships. They include media companies like PBL, Internet Service Providers like America Online, telecommunications companies like Telstra, some large, established, Internet retailers like Amazon.com, large banks like the CBA and even, distributors like Australia Post.

Broad-band digital broadcasting, which starts in Australia in the year 2001, will enable the Internet to be received on television sets, so further expanding the reach of business. This is because, in the year 2000, although nearly every home in Australia has a TV, fewer than half of the 6 million homes in Australia have a PC and less than one quarter of homes have access to the Internet. However, even now, forty percent of adults access the Internet. More will do so as computers become increasingly user-friendly with, for instance, such features as voice activation instead of keyboard control.

Guaranteed security and privacy for transactions and trustworthy, reliable service will be fundamental considerations for commerce service providers (CSPs) who wish to retain the loyalty of customers. There is already evidence to suggest that customers, having grown to expect a rapid, efficient service are likely to be particularly intolerant of interruptions to service. This will mean that all CSPs will need to develop and maintain expensive back-up systems and highly sophisticated defences against industrial sabotage.

❑ Internet Fallout

There is debate about the effect e-commerce will have on regular businesses. There are some that believe that the Internet will eventually take advertising revenue away from newspapers and magazines. It could well be that, as the Internet is adopted by more people, such functions as dating agencies will move to the web. However, in the short term, at least, as web sites attempt to attract more visitors, advertising revenues in newspapers and magazines have increased considerably.

" No company, big or small, is immune to strong and dangerous competition from some tiny, unknown organisation on the other side of the world. **"**

SOME OLD WORLD TO E-WORLD TRANSITIONS

☆ Main Point

The Internet is likely to permanently change the way many people conduct their lives and how many companies do business. The Internet hosts an unbelievable concentration of information. It has changed the way we communicate with each other and it has made things cheaper to buy and manufacture.

❝ To succeed in Internet sales you need to exploit the unique advantages it has over selling in the physical world. **❞**

✓ Executive Summary

The adoption of the Internet by business and the general public promises to change the way we purchase many goods and services and the way we obtain information. Listed below are just a selection of sites or services that have made the news over the past year. As long as you know what you are looking for and have some strategy for finding it the Internet provides a lot of useful information. There are sites dealing with specialised topics like law and wine, as well as those providing access to on-line encyclopaedias. The Internet allows us to make contact with people we know (from Internet cafes) and those we don't (Dating Agencies). Busy professionals like doctors can keep in contact with colleagues and up to date with developments in medicine. We can buy things like wine, toys and music over the Internet at bargain prices. The Internet also allows companies like car manufacturers to improve the efficiency with which they conduct their business. However, some goods and services that require inspection, like real estate, are not so likely to move totally to the Internet.

❖ Some Newsworthy Examples of Internet Developments

❏ Dating Agencies

Finding a compatible partner has always been a case of hit or miss. For busy people, shy people or those who want to meet a lot of people in a short time, dating agencies might prove useful. But, with high introduction fees and a wide variability in quality of service, many dating agency customers have become disillusioned. Now, introduction agencies have moved to the Internet and are able to extend and customise their service while, at the same time, dramatically reducing their fees by making the system interactive and fully automated. Clients at Soulmates, for instance, can join for free and have access to a large data base of profiles of people from around the world with introductions costing as little as $4 each. The company seems to be making a profit as well with revenues reported to be as much as $40 000 a month.

☐ Music

It is very hard for a rock band to be adopted by a record label. In the US a band has to typically cut its own CD and sell 5000 copies before a recording company will even look at it. However a top end personal computer with the right software is now capable of carrying out multi tracking, sequences and mixing thus allowing bands to record cheaply. They can then promote their music globally over the Internet. Of course there is still a problem for the band to be 'discovered' by fans even if they post their CD for listening at a free site like MP3.com or for sale on, say, Amazon.com. There are simply so many bands out there that it is difficult to become noticed let alone become popular. However, if a band is able to sell a few thousand copies of its CD it can start to make money. By the same token, the Internet is a cornucopia for music lovers, because there is so much out there that is free to listen to and down-load.

☐ Internet Cafes

A new type of business has emerged in the last five or so years. Even in small towns, especially ones with tourists, you'll find an Internet cafe. They are useful, especially for travellers wanting to keep in touch with home. Although some still stick to a formula of coffee and high speed Internet PCs others have changed their service to meet the needs of the local demographic. If travellers are the predominant customers they may find the service includes fax and international phone call booths and a 'post restante' mailing address. If students are the most common customers the services may emphasise scanning, photocopying and word processing. If business people form the bulk of custom, services may include document binding, large print runs, digital scanning, a conference room and even teleconferencing.

❒ Cars

Used cars can already be bought and sold over the Internet in Australia. Now Ford customers can order a limited range of high performance vehicles over the Internet then visit one of twelve specialised Australian dealerships to confirm the order. Ford Australia will monitor the success of the site to determine the feasibility of offering its whole range on-line. Car manufacturers must tread carefully here for fear of alienating the dealerships that currently provide the outlet for the sale of their vehicles.

Nevertheless both Ford and GM are embracing the Internet in a big way by both announcing that their entire supply chains for the purchase of parts for vehicles will be conducted over the Internet. This is a massive undertaking for both companies with Ford, for instance, dealing with 30 000 suppliers worldwide. It is expected that the move will result in dramatic savings on procurement and inventory with shorter production times. This should result in less expensive cars being made to order and delivered to customers within days.

❒ Wine

Companies selling wine over the Internet have benefited from the fact that many Australians have already bought wine by the dozen, sight unseen, from mail order wine clubs. Internet wine sellers have the advantage of offering their customers a wide choice of wines at prices that are less than in physical stores. Wineplanet.com.au only started its current web site in March 1999 but is now the biggest seller of wines over the Internet with between 4000 and 5000 wines on site and a tracking service for other wines. The site provides advice on wines by experienced writers, a wine lovers club, free delivery to most capital cities and plans to add gourmet foods, beer and cigars this year. Recognising that many potential purchasers baulk at providing credit card details over the Internet, the company also lets customers pay by cheque, phone or fax (toll free). Although the current leader, Wineplanet will face competition from other companies including Coles Supermarkets but it hopes to keep ahead of the pack with its 'first mover advantage'.

☐ Toys

Perhaps the biggest thing going for Internet toy vendors is that customers, usually adults, often do not know what toys to buy for a child. Physical toy stores, especially at Christmas time, are very busy and help and advice is often not readily available. An Internet store, on the other hand can help the customer make a choice by putting products into age categories and including detailed descriptions of each toy. But there are disadvantages to selling toys over the net. Packages can be heavy and bulky meaning delivery charges can be high and, because many toys are bought for Christmas or a birthday, they also have to be delivered by a certain date if the customer is to be happy with the service. It is yet to be seen how well the Internet toy business will perform. Experience with Internet toy sales in the US has been mixed with some stores doing very good business and others pulling out altogether.

☐ Experts and Opinions

Sites that attract many eyeballs can charge advertisers for ads at their site. Since information is king and there are many people seeking it, it stands to reason that sites providing information might succeed on the Internet. For instance, the US site, 'Epinions', attracts visitors by presenting itself as a guide for shoppers. It solicits and posts on its web site reviews by the general public about products and services such as computers, electronic equipment, finance, food, drink and travel. Viewers can see what others think of an item before committing themselves to a purchase. The site receives income from advertising and deals with on-line retailers. The review of a new product might be linked to a store selling it, for instance. The site organisers also plan to pay individuals for highly rated reviews. Other sites like advoco.com, About.com and ExpertCentral provide access to expert advice on a wide range of topics. Ask.com attempts to provide an answer to a question entered in plain language such as "What places should I visit in Australia?"

☐ Medicine

Although they are busy people, doctors need to keep up with the latest in diagnostics and treatment of patients. An Internet service run by Med-E-Serv is designed to meet that need. The site provides medical professionals with the opportunity of gaining free access to 12 000 health professionals in Australia and New Zealand. The site also offers fast Internet access and Forums for communicating with colleagues. Perhaps the most popular components of the service are discussion groups on a wide variety of topics of interest to doctors such as pain relief or asthma treatment. Rather than operating the discussions in real time, participants contribute, at their leisure, to the thread of ideas controlled by a moderator.

☐ Real Estate

The current wisdom about Internet selling is that goods and services that are clearly defined or have a recognisable brand such as computers are easier to sell than such things as clothing which often need to be inspected closely and touched. So it is little wonder that, at the moment at least, real estate sites are used as sources of research by house buyers but the vast majority of people still feel the need to make a physical inspection of a property before purchase. Nor have real estate auctions over the Internet been very successful. This is partly because the technology connecting web participants with the auction site is still relatively primitive and because Australian law prohibits live, on-line bidding, leaving bidders no alternative but to bid by phone.

☐ Law

Some law companies are offering on-line legal services to clients at rates that are reputedly less than for face-to-face consultations. One company offers conveyancing on-line and suggests that customers can save time using it, especially in the initial stages of a house sale. Another will draft documents for clients and allows customers to download, for a fee, documents such as a will proforma or a confidentiality agreement. Other sites are providing a service to lawyers by making provision for the electronic filing of documents, setting of trial dates and preparation of appeal books. The site

are charging and adjust prices accordingly. A list of customers together with personal details and buying preferences has become a very saleable item in e-commerce. Customer Data Mapping can also involve gathering information about the spending habits and needs of a customer (data mining) so that the customer can be better serviced, and, of course, the vendor can make more sales. Good customers, for instance, would be identified and provided with special privileges.

An e-tailer will not succeed without great customer service. This means more than cheaper product, quicker processing or access to a greater range of stock. It means a service where customers get the feeling that their special needs are being looked after - service is customised. We are also seeing organisations exploiting the fact that they have a large number of regular visitors by opening portals. They sell space in an Internet shopping mall to vendors who know that their store is likely to receive more potential shoppers through the portal. Auctions have also taken off on the Internet, some auction houses having inventories of half a million or so items at any one time. Buyers like the sites because they can pick up bargains. Items that are clearly defined, like airline tickets or brand name clothing sell well because trust in getting what you pay for can be high.

E-tailing has had major ramifications for certain businesses. Courier services have benefited from the increased need for the delivery of goods to customers from Internet sales. Some manufacturers have decided that they can make better profits by selling directly to the public, bypassing retailers. This has understandably been met with a backlash from retail store owners. Groceries can now be bought over the Internet for the convenience of busy families. With the added charges for packing and delivery it is doubtful whether this will become the predominant form of grocery shopping in the foreseeable future.

❖ The Big Ideas

❒ Convergence

The term convergence means the joining together of a number of things to make a new entity. There are at least three distinctly different subsets of this definition. Convergence can mean:

(A) 'Clicks & Bricks'; a company that has combined both physical retailing and e-tailing.

(B) Synergistic Mergers: the joining together of two or more companies to form a bigger company that can benefit from the different strengths of the merged companies.

(C) A Merging of Devices: a merging of the functions of hitherto different devices to produce a device that has multi-function capabilities (see Morphing Mobiles).

(A) Clicks & Bricks

❝ It's not an easy business to get into, people underestimate the costs involved in setting up a user-friendly, up-to-date Website and the infrastructure to provide the deliveries. **❞**

Doug Carlson, managing director, Greengrocer.com, quoted by Karen Milliner, The Courier Mail, 17/7/99.

The Internet revolution took traditional retailers by surprise back in the mid-90s. A whole new way of buying attracted Internet-savvy individuals and clever on-line retailers soon captured a significant market share in some retail sectors such as computers, books and CDs. Sizeable discounts were offered by e-tailers undercutting traditional stores selling the same product. Some of the larger retailers have taken some time to respond to this challenge and, near the end of the 90s, Y2K compliance issues occupied time and money. Now companies are freed of that burden we should expect large bricks-and-mortar organisations to begin to challenge Internet upstarts. It is true that developing a user-friendly Internet retail site does not come cheaply. But established retail companies have the ability to compete. Most of them already make a profit (something that can not be said for a good many e-tailers) and already have recognised brands and loyal customers. They have an established infrastructure of shops and warehouses, large inventories, a wide choice of products, an established distribution system and, if necessary, can outsource the distribution of goods.

Return of goods has been a major problem with Internet sales. The fact that large retailers have bricks and mortar stores will make return of goods a lot easier for many customers. Bricks and mortar vendors have the added advantage of being able to integrate their Internet selling with their traditional business. For instance, if a price change is made in their retail store they have the ability to simultaneously and automatically alter the price of the same item sold on-line. It is therefore likely that, because of their size, they will survive as 'clicks and mortar' stores. The Youth Hostels Association of Australia and Thrifty car rentals have both reported considerable increases in sales as a result of opening a web presence. It is interesting that they both have known 'brand names' and services for budget minded travellers. Both companies' e-sites are easy-to-navigate and bookings can be placed without immediate payment.

Some big names have made a move onto the net. Nike has finally relented and given permission for a sporting goods dealer to sell its goods over the net. General Motors also plans to sell cars over the Internet. However, Toyota, Australia stopped the direct selling of cars on-line in October 1999 citing poor volume of sales, the antipathy of car dealerships and the reticence of customers to pay more than a deposit on the Internet. Levi Strauss once was the talk of the e-tailer set with its web site giving visitors the opportunity to provide their measurements over the Internet so that jeans could be custom-made for them. However, late in 1999 they decided to no longer sell directly over the Internet leaving sales to established bricks and mortar and Internet retailers.

Some companies, after developing a web presence, have opened one or more bricks and mortar stores. Others have formed alliances with companies selling from existing bricks and mortar stores. This strategy allows customers to return goods, talk with a salesperson, touch goods and provides further exposure of the Internet brand name to potential customers. Indeed the trend seems to be emerging where many retailers see the benefits of having both a physical and an Internet presence. They are unsure whether shoppers will use the Internet to merely gather information about products then go to a physical store to make their purchase or whether they will complete the purchase over the net. Their choice will probably depend on a number of factors such as the type of product sought and the experience of the consumer. Reports, however, indicate that the increase of Internet business has had an impact on some bricks and mortar stores. In the US some shopping mall landlords have prohibited all advertising of on-line sales in their stores. Other landlords have taken the opposite view and welcomed the Internet by providing computers with Internet access in their malls and inviting consumers to research products on-line then make their purchases in the mall.

There are two points of view about what types of companies will eventually remain as viable businesses on the Internet when higher interest rates, possible decline in customer confidence, takeovers or a host of other factors may cause many Internet companies to perish. One view suggests that, because setting up a good site and attracting customers is so expensive to do, those that developed an early and significant presence on the Internet will be the ones that flourish. The second point of view has it that, although many traditional companies have been slow to open Internet sites, the very fact that they are already profitable, have established sales and distribution systems, loyal customers and recognised brand names, will allow them to build fast. They can learn from the mistakes of early pioneers and might eventually overtake the upstarts.

(B) Synergistic Mergers

A second meaning of the term 'convergence' is the merging together of two or more companies to form a new conglomeration that exploits the assets each of the companies brings to the combination. Sectors that might form synergies include portals like Yahoo, commercial sites like Amazon, ISPs like America Online (AOL) and media companies like News Corporation. A recent example was the proposed merger between (AOL), the world's largest Internet provider, and Time Warner, the world's largest media and entertainment company. The combination is likely to bring more news and a wide range of entertainment to the Internet. Put another way, the Internet will provide another outlet for entertainment and news. It would seem that businesses are realising that, in order to compete in the new commercial environment, size is important. Rather than do it all themselves they merge, form alliances or take over other companies in an effort to consolidate a better position to exploit opportunities and economies of scale in the new worlds of e-commerce, worldwide communication and entertainment.

(C) Merging Devices

A third meaning of the term 'convergence' is the merging or 'morphing' of devices such as mobile phones, computers, electronic organisers and televisions into multi-functional communication devices taking advantage of technologies like the Internet. Such combinations promise a new raft of possibilities for communication and entertainment including, for instance, access to overseas TV programs. (see Morphing Mobiles)

❏ Approaches to Selling on the Internet

Freebies for Information

The cliché 'Information is Power' is no more valid than on the Internet. People selling on the Internet want to target buyers for their products. It therefore stands to reason that those organisations that already have large numbers of regular visitors can charge vendors for the privilege of advertising at their site. The site thus becomes an Internet portal.

> **"** We can offer a cheaper product on-line because customers do some of the work. **"**

Some Internet portal sites offer free e-mail (or freemail) in return for filling in a survey about their interests and other personal details such as age, gender and income. Portals use the survey material to attract advertisers to their sites. When freemail users open their e-mail they are presented with an array of advertising, often customised to their particular interests. Free e-mail users typically check daily for messages. Portal site owners hope that the user will also use one of the many other services provided by the site such as shopping or searching for information. As competition between portals offering freemail increases, they have found the need to offer additional free services, such as address books and calendars, to maintain customer loyalty. It is yet to be seen how effective this strategy is in providing revenue for advertisers. Free services are most likely to attract newcomers and lower income Internet users. There is a question, about how much this group is likely to spend on Internet purchases.

Some companies have merely transferred existing ways of doing business to the Internet. For instance, one site in Australia (www.shopfree.com.au) provides a service to businesses that wish to offer free samples or brochures and catalogues of their products. The theory behind the strategy is that, once a potential customer has sampled the product, they are more likely to purchase it. The site makes money by charging companies for the privilege of advertising their wares at the site.

> **"** Adopting e-commerce is like opening a big store in an expensive shopping mall. It might not hugely increase profits but it exposes you in another public arena and helps you keep up with the opposition. **"**

At least one company in the US has offered to loan computers to selected individuals who are prepared to divulge a raft of personal information. The computer is set up so that advertisements (which are periodically updated) appear on the screen each time individuals use their computers. Revenue is expected to come from advertisers paying for the right to promote their products in the advertisements. Another US company provides free computers and free Internet access to selected customers who, in return, must spend a certain amount of money on Internet shopping each month. If they fail to spend the money on shopping they will be billed for the hire of the computer and Internet access services.

Yet another company provides customers with access to a worldwide message service for the price of a local phone call. The system will only work if the company, Talkstar, has set up a computer server in the caller's local telephone area. Already established in the US, Talkstar plans to introduce the system to Australia. Talkstar obtains its revenue from companies that place their advertisements on the company's servers. Each time individuals phone the server to collect their messages they must listen to advertisements before being able to listen to their voicemail messages. Free fax is available from other companies.

☐ Providing Great Service

In physical stores shoppers appreciate good service. Preferably they want service that is immediate. A shop assistant that is friendly and knowledgeable about their product range will sell more goods. By analogy, good service in e-tailing means a web site that loads quickly, is easily navigable, gets you the service or information you require, provides good security, looks good and gives you access to help if you need it.

In a competitive e-tailing world it is important to provide the surfer with a good shopping experience. For instance, some bookshops on the Internet provide a list of the books they sell. This is all right if you know the name of the book you want. But what if you have a topic and need the title of a good book? Amazon.com provides the extra information to help you in your search. Not only does it have an efficient search engine but it provides a reader rating of the various options, provides reviews by other readers, indicates other books bought by buyers of a book and, in most cases, indicates the approximate lag time between ordering and shipment. This added information is invaluable to the purchaser and could lead to more purchases than the visitor originally intended. Amazon.com also offers an enormous range of books, at a discount, from a site that is easy to navigate and with pages fast to load. All this adds up to a user-friendly service.

Another innovation involving the Internet is called Permission Marketing. It involves a company placing advertisements either in the print media or on-line offering individuals the chance to win something, by playing a game or taking part in a competition. In return the company provides them with information about its products. If individuals agree to take part they have given the company 'permission' to 'educate' them about how the company could be of service to them. Typically the game lasts several weeks during which time individuals receive a number of e-mails a week as part of the game. At the same time they receive information about products. After completion of the game, sales people may follow up with clients. The theory is that a client will become loyal to a seller if the seller is able to personalise the service and customise the product to the needs of the individual.

☐ Portals

A portal is a sophisticated Internet site that attracts large numbers of visitors who are able to browse through and purchase goods and services from a wide range of vendors who pay the portal for the privilege of being exposed to so many visitors. Examples of portals are Telstra BigPond, Ozemail, Compuserve, Looksmart and ninemsn. Internet heavyweights like Excite, Yahoo and Amazon.com have, for some time offered portals to Internet shopping malls. They are exploiting the fact that they have millions of regular visitors to their own sites. They can offer the potential buying power of these visitors to sellers of a wide range of products and services.

Some portal operators are offering, to all shops in their mall, a reliable system for processing payment and shipping of goods. So a customer who buys goods at a number of stores only pays on leaving the portal. The portal operator collects payment for all the stores then distributes payments to the stores (less its commission). Portals offer more than just acting as the checkout operator. They can keep statistics on purchases and collect feedback about stores. They can also offer incentive programs for visitors to their portal. However, many retailers are reticent to sign up with a portal because the high cost of developing an on-line presence increases further when fees have to be paid to the portal operator.

It is likely that a new generation of portals will provide the public not only with access to e-mail and the Internet. They will also provide, for hire, from a central server, all desktop software, freeing the customer from the regular purchase of new software and upgrades and providing personalised products on demand.

☐ Auctions

Internet auctions provide a new way of buying items at bargain prices. Anyone can visit an auction site to see what is on offer. They only need to register if they decide to sell or bid on an item. A seller posts a description of their item or items, perhaps with a photograph. The closing date for bids is declared, typically a week or more hence. The reserve price is declared. The successful purchaser will have exceeded the reserve price and be the highest bidder in the set time. The host of the auction site collects a posting fee, and a commission of between 1.25 and 5 percent of the sale price from the seller. After the auction is complete the seller and successful purchaser make contact to arrange payment in return for delivery of the goods. Some sites offer to act as an intermediary between seller and buyer by accepting payment from the buyer and releasing the balance of the purchase price (after fee and commission have been deducted) only when the purchaser has received the goods. Reverse on-line auctions are different. They allow customers to declare what they want to buy and have suppliers give their best price.

If a seller has a number of identical items (lets say six) for sale, purchasers can compete in a Dutch auction. This involves buyers nominating a price and saying how many of the items they wish to buy. At the end of the sale the six highest bidders would purchase the goods at a price equal to the bid of the sixth highest successful bidder. Internet auctions work well for buyers who know a lot about what they are buying such as computer hardware and software, car parts, furniture, books, niche collectables like stamps, rooms in hotels and airline tickets. Most transactions on Internet auction sites have so far been between private consumers but a lot more money is likely to be made by sites that offer a business-to-consumer service (such as those selling new 'shrink-wrapped' items, prestige used cars, works of art and antique furniture). Transactions between businesses are also likely to become more important.

But on-line auction houses are legally prohibited from selling certain items including human body parts like hearts, shares, pharmaceutical drugs, weapons and endangered animals.

A number of auction sites have been established in Australia. As with other Internet ventures they are likely to face strong competition from established American on-line auction houses, like eBay, that choose to open a local service in Australia. It is likely that all but the biggest auction houses will tend to specialise, either in certain categories of item or servicing specific geographic areas. Buying locally is more attractive to consumers rather than from someone in a distant city. Commentators predict that the Australian market can only support two or three auction sites and these are likely to be the busiest sites, ones that have plenty of inventory and attracting lots of buyers. So auction sites need to advertise in conventional arenas such as billboards and newspapers.

❑ Other Issues

Delivering the Goods: Order Processing & Distribution

The biggest winners of the e-commerce revolution may not be those who sell products or services. Instead, it could be those who conduct the complex and demanding task of making sure that customers get their goods quickly and vendors get paid for their product. Two types of company are in this business; those who process orders and those who deliver the goods. There are some companies that specialise in what are known as 'back-end' order-processing operations. They may research and select the product that gives best value for money. They will ensure timely ordering. They will track orders and keep customers informed of progress and they will handle payments. They could also handle returns and replacements.

Express courier companies will also be in increasing demand as e-commerce expands to encompass the world. Established international couriers, like FedEx, UPS and TNT combine both order processing and delivery. They not only provide fast, reliable transport but allow customers to book a job on-line, track and trace packages and obtain proof of delivery, in real time. By entering the details of the package at the courier web site a customer can find out its current location. When business-to-business commerce increases they will benefit even more. They will, for instance, be able to provide logistical and warehousing services to any company needing to provide a rapid response to Internet orders.

From July 1, 2000 Australia Post (AP) faces competition from private providers in the delivery of larger letters and all international mail. However, with over 4000 postal outlets in Australia, AP stands to benefit from the mushrooming of business in delivery of Internet orders. As household mail declines AP expects to increase its share of business mail. Already profitable, AP plans to update its delivery technology by introducing bar coding for business letters, something FedEx did for packages over twenty years ago. By October 2000 AP expects to have started a web-based bill payment system which will be also linked to an Internet Fulfilment Service including warehousing, distribution, tracking and delivery services for on-line retailers. Although AP has not indicated that it will adopt the system, a US company, Stamps.com, has developed a method for purchase of postage over the Internet. Consumers in the US can buy postage on-line from Stamps.com by using a credit card. Stamps.com then prints the name and address and needed postage onto the consumer's printer in an encoded format to prevent fraud.

Security & Authentication

> " There is still a lot of distrust of the net. So people look for the security of dealing with companies they know and brands that they recognise. "

Being sure who is on the other side of your Internet connection is one of the major problems of e-commerce at the moment. Smart cards (see Smart Cards) will be able to carry authentication by way of a digital certificate, an electronic 'signature' by which an individual can confidently identify an on-line purchaser or vendor. They have been available for four years in Australia from reputable third parties, but very few companies have adopted their use. At the moment credit card transactions are the predominant form of money transfer over the Internet and can be open to fraud, although it is probably safer to use them over the net than elsewhere.

Advertising

Television and newspaper owners are among the strongest investors in Internet business. Because they are already in the business of information gathering and dissemination they have an advantage over many other industries. Although reports indicate little change yet, some commentators predict that the advent of on-line stores and auctions will eventually have an impact on the income derived by newspaper publishers from classified advertisements. Perhaps at greater risk are publications that specialise in consumer-to-consumer sales advertising, such as free issue local newspapers. These are likely to be carried and processed more conveniently over the Internet. Some studies also report that heavy users of the Internet are less likely to watch television or buy papers, further cutting into the sales of newspapers. On the other hand, there are so many web sites today that they must find ways of advertising their presence. Billboards, radio, TV and newspaper campaigns are ways of attracting people to a site. So it is not surprising that some newspapers have lately reported an increase in advertising revenue from web companies advertising their sites.

◻ Industry Foci

Selling Computers

Traditionally computer makers have manufactured computers and sent them to retailers who sold them to customers. Then Dell Computers began taking orders from customers over the Internet, putting together customised machines and sending them directly to the customer. The customer was a winner, buying a very good machine that was delivered quickly and at a competitive price. Freight delivery companies, benefiting from increased custom, were also winners. But there were also losers. Rival computer companies like IBM and Hewlett-Packard began to lose market share. So they decided to also sell directly to the public. As a result sales by some retailers have declined. This has been exacerbated by the advent of Internet portal sites that put visitors in contact with companies like Hewlett-Packard who then sell directly to the customer.

In June 1999, apparently in an attempt to counter direct selling by manufacturers, the biggest retailer of computers in Australia, Harvey Norman was reported, to have said that it would not sell computers made by companies that also sell directly to the public. (BRW, 4/6/99). In August 1999 (The Australian, 31/8/99) Compaq, the world's largest manufacturer of personal computers indicated it would open its own branded stores and a call centre and also sell computers directly to the public over the Internet. As a result, Harvey Norman was reported to have terminated its contract with Compaq to sell Compaq

" We won't need middlemen any more! **"**

computers in Harvey Norman stores. In September 1999 Harvey Norman was reported (The Australian 13/9/99) to be opening an Internet selling site for its products before the Christmas sales season. In November 1999 (The Australian Financial Review, 8/11/99) IBM, falling behind Compaq and Dell in sales, announced that it would sell its PCs only over the Internet. This would allow IBM to sell PCs at low margins but, at the same time, increase sales of software and such items as monitors as well as finance packages. This is a model followed by Hewlett-Packard that sells computers and printers but makes more profit from refills for its printers.

Dell Computer Corporation has been described by Fortune magazine (September 1999) as the company that has developed 'the best example of a new business paradigm' (BRW, 16/11/99). Dell uses a combination of tele-marketing, advertising and face-to-face selling for its products. But Dell has been successful by doing much more than selling customised computers directly to the public. It has mastered the art of supply chain logistics. Suppliers of parts are kept fully aware of the variations in demand for product and can adjust next day's delivery of parts to the factory door (in Malaysia, Ireland, China and the US) accordingly. This has helped the company keep stored inventory to a minimum and reduce its manufacturing throughput time to between five and six hours, easily beating its competitors and dramatically reducing costs. Such fast throughput means that the company has little backlog of inventory and can clear the assembly line and quickly start the manufacture of a new product if necessary.

Selling Groceries

" Decide fast! **"**

Coles Supermarkets and Woolworths' Supermarkets together control two thirds of the grocery business in Australia and, in a business of small margins they are always alert for some new competitive advantage. The latest development in their battle has involved in-store banking with Woolworths forming an exclusive agreement with the Commonwealth Bank and Coles forming alliances with eight financial institutions and introducing unbranded ATMs to many stores. It is expected that this is the first step towards Internet grocery shopping with smart cards and sophisticated ordering, delivery and tracking systems. This is likely to include increased on-line communication with suppliers about customer buying trends so that each individual store can fill shelves with products that meet the needs of their local buying public.

Typically a customer who currently e-mails a shopping list to a big chain like Woolworths or Coles can expect to pay a fee for someone to gather and pack the goods on the grocery list and another fee for delivery. This will typically add about $14 to a $100 grocery order. Another company, ShopFast, has no inventory, but instead buys product from a wholesaler, packs shopping lists and delivers for the cost of product plus a small delivery fee. Because fulfilling the order is time consuming, it is unlikely that grocers will ever be able to drop the packing and delivery charge. This makes grocery shopping relatively expensive over the Internet. So Internet grocery shopping is unlikely to become as widespread as, for instance, buying a CD over the Internet, which is cheaper and much faster than going to a retail store. However, for the harried professional class it will be an attractive way of freeing time for leisure.

Some companies have started Internet grocery stores from scratch but the costs are enormous if they are to fulfil their promise of accurate and rapid delivery. For instance, Webvan, a US Internet grocer, promises delivery within a half hour timeframe if the order is five hours old. In order to fulfil this promise, Webvan, has had to invest in high-tech inventory and distribution systems including large warehouses around the country. Other Internet grocers have decided to remain relatively small so that they do not over-extend their capacity to deliver and can keep current customers happy.

" The future is so uncertain, the competition so intense that, although we've been on the top of the heap for some time we could be made irrelevant at any time. **"**

For all such grocery companies customers must be presented with an on-line service that is quick, easy-to-use and stress free. Most potential customers are first likely to go to a site for a browse. If they like what they see they want to be able to sign up for the service without hassle. Then the goods need to be easily located and identified on site. Some sites do this a lot better than others and this will affect the amount of custom a site attracts. Even so, if you are looking for choice there is likely to be less on-line than in a 'bricks-and-mortar' store.

Large bricks-and-mortar retail outlets like Coles are following a US trend and outsourcing the fulfilment part of their on-line business. In the case of Coles it is likely to be Australia Post that will deliver to the customer's door. Coles-Myer are also exploiting the fact that busy professional people and generation X-ers want nutritious food that they do not need to cook themselves. Let's Eat stores provide both eat-in and take-away foods and wines for the upper end of the buying public. Starting in Melbourne and Sydney, it is expected that the concept will expand to other cities if things go well.

GLOBALISATION

☆ Main Point

Globalisation, fed by cheap, fast transport and communication, is such a key feature of contemporary change that it has the potential to affect many aspects of our lives.

✓ Executive Summary

Cheap transportation and communication, along with the freeing of international trade by the elimination of many tariffs, has led to a surge in the internationalisation of business. Some companies have expanded to foreign shores. Others have set out to expand through acquisitions or mergers. With markets, worldwide opening up, companies see the need to place their stake in foreign lands or lose in the global gold rush.

Australia is one country that should benefit from globalisation. With a small domestic market it has long been outward looking and has experience in international trade. It is also ahead of many countries in its adoption of the Internet and should be able to take advantage of the predicted boom in e-commerce over the next few years. It is also placed close to exciting markets in the Asia-Pacific region, a fact that should make it a place for multi-nationals to set up as a foothold in the region. Its time zone position also makes it a favourable site for collaboration on 24 hour-7 day a week business needs. But globalisation is of concern to some. There are those who fear that jobs will be lost if they have to compete with cheap overseas labour.

> **"** The average Australian family is about $1000 better off, thanks to trade liberalisation and increasing globalisation. **"**
>
> Peter Charlton & Graham Lloyd, The Courier Mail, 14/11/98.

❖ The Big Ideas

❏ Why Globalisation?

Globalisation involves the internationalisation of trade, investment, ownership and services. This has meant that national borders become of little relevance. Globalisation has come about through a number of technologies increasing in importance, becoming cheaper and more universally available. Since 1850 the cost of transportation has steadily decreased making it more and more easy to send goods around the world.

**" The two litre
double overhead
cam engine is
Australian. The
automatic transmission,
developed by ZF, is
German. The sleek
Italian styling is
courtesy of one of the
world's most famous
automotive designers,
Giorgetto Giugiaro,
of the Ital Design
studio. Add to these
British expertise in
noise and vibration
reduction, from MIRA.
Suspension-tuning
was developed by
Lotus, also in the UK.
With state-of-the-art
automation at
Daewoo's Korean
manufacturing plant
bringing it all
together. "**

Advertisement for the
Daewoo Leganza, 1998.

**" Asia, with a huge
number of young
consumers, is
potentially a very
lucrative market. "**

Since the early 1990s the price of worldwide communication began to drop and, with the advent of the Internet, communication between everyone in the developed world has become inexpensive. Lastly, the increased dismantling of protection of markets, over the last 25 years, has resulted in increased efficiencies (and the demise of inefficient systems) in the world economy. These three factors combined, having compressed time, space and markets, have led to a headlong rush by companies to create worldwide commercial empires.

❐ Approaches to Globalisation

There are at least two ways of viewing commercial globalisation. One view of globalisation is of a company that has proved itself successful in the domestic market deciding to compete on the world market and sell its products or services overseas. Another view of globalisation is of a company that has strong domestic success deciding to make acquisitions of or seeking mergers with similar companies overseas. For instance, a Swedish lock company, Assa Abloy has, over the past six years, made over twenty acquisitions of foreign lock companies including the Australian company, Lockwood. It now owns six per cent of the world's lock market. It is this latter approach to globalisation (mergers, acquisitions and alliances) that multinational organisations seem to be favouring. Those in the information technology and telecommunications industries see the importance of developing global networks for their services. They are entering into a period of frenzied activity. They also see a world where phones, TVs and the Internet are all merged into one polymorphous information-entertainment-commercial service to the world. So the flurry of mergers, alliances and acquisitions is likely to continue for some time to come.

❐ Global-local Advertising

Once they have established a global market, multinational corporations face the task of making sure that their advertising programs are culturally appropriate for each local market. Some Australian consumers, for instance, might not be attracted to products advertised in contexts or by people from overseas. On the other hand, companies that focus on the youth market exploit the fact that many young people around the world aspire to a United States led uniformity.

❒ Cheaper Imports

The average Australian should be able to buy foreign goods much more cheaply than their parents had at the same age. This is because there has been a slow but inexorable reduction in import tariffs on foreign goods, designed originally to protect domestic industries. Farm equipment, cars, clothing and shoes are all relatively cheaper than they were twenty or so years ago.

❒ Employment Fears

There are some who believe, however, that, if multinational corporations dominate the world through globalisation, the world will exist as a 20:80 society where multinational companies and the small workforces integral to their success (the 20%) are the major beneficiaries. The remaining 80% of the world's workforce would be either unemployed, underemployed or are part of a large but relatively poorly paid service community. Perhaps, with this as a possible future scenario, it is understandable that, while American corporations are busy competing for their share of global markets, the American public is unsure whether globalisation is such a good thing. Americans fear for their jobs because their products might have to compete with products made by cheap labour overseas. They also fear that international agreements like the Kyoto agreement on global greenhouse gas emissions will force companies to reduce productivity which might put pressure on jobs.

❒ The E-Commerce Race

Because of its technological head start, the size of its domestic consumer market and its willingness to experiment, the US is ahead of the rest of the world in terms of e-commerce. Currently three quarters of all e-commerce originates in the US. Use of the Internet in many European countries has been hampered by the fact that local telephone calls are charged by the minute. Asia is further behind than Europe. Japan has, hitherto, been slow to embrace the Internet. China has great potential but has only a small percentage of Internet users.

Australia is more advanced than many of these countries and should be able to exploit its position close to Asian markets.

> " ...the defining anxiety in globalisation is fear of rapid change from an enemy you can't see, touch or feel- a sense that your job, community or workplace can be changed at any moment by anonymous economic and technological forces that are anything but stable. "
>
> Thomas Friedman (1999). The Lexus and the Olive Tree, London, Harper Collins.

> " Instead of exploiting the possibilities of globalisation Australian companies might find themselves the takeover target of expanding global empires. "

> **"** The shopping habits of a nineteen-year-old Londoner may be more similar to those of a nineteen-year-old in Rio than those of a 22-year-old Londoner. **"**

For instance, with its multicultural background, Australia is likely to provide a base for 'back-office' work for the Asia-Pacific. With its comparatively low cost of doing business, Australia is also a country of choice for many multinational companies wanting to expand into the Asia-Pacific region. The cost of running a business in the US is fifty percent greater than in Australia. In Japan, it is two and a half times as expensive as Australia.

☐ Time Zone Advantages

Australia also benefits from its time zone. Let us say, for example, that a company wishes to develop a product as quickly as possible. Traditionally, this has meant dividing a development team into three shifts that work, at the same site, around the clock. But now, through the miracle of e-mail an alternative mode of operation presents itself. A team in Los Angeles can start work at 9am and work until 5pm. By that time it is 9am in Brisbane and a hand-over of the task to the Brisbane team, by e-mail, can take place. The Brisbane team works until 5pm by which time it is 7am in London. The task is transferred to the London team that then works until 3pm by which time it is ready to transfer back to the Los Angeles team for the cycle to continue, each team fresh from a good night's sleep. By the same means, financial markets need never sleep with some exchange somewhere, open in every 24-hour period.

☐ Control of Global Trade

> **"** Large multinationals can now dictate some of the decisions made by small and medium-sized nations. **"**

With increasing international trade, nations, from time to time, will come into dispute with each other. The World Trade Organisation was formed to set international rules for trade and facilitate the free flow of trade between nations. Since many nations have their own unique currencies, many of them floating rather than being tied to a fixed exchange rate, the International Monetary Fund (IMF) is there to maintain stability in world currency markets. The World Bank also helps the poorest nations with investments to improve economic growth.

BUSINESS-TO-BUSINESS TRANSACTIONS OVER THE INTERNET (B2B)

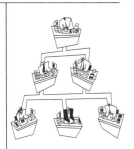

☆ Main Point

There will be an explosive uptake of Internet support services by all levels and types of business over the next three years that will forever change the way business is done.

☐ Executive Summary

Business-to-business Internet transactions will make the majority of businesses more efficient by improving management, financial control, manufacture, sales, human resource management and logistics. Businesses will purchase the software and training to support this revolution from application service providers. Businesses will be able to purchase or lease integrated systems or choose separate applications from a 'best of breed' source.

At the same time, avenues for the sale or purchase of goods have increased. Goods and services can now be sold/bought through portals consisting of a collection of 'shops' to which the portal owner attracts visitors (see e-sales). Or a business could join forces with others in the same industry to attract favourable prices by buying or selling in bulk. On-line auctions provide a way for businesses to sell surplus stock. On-line Exchanges will work like stock exchanges but with goods and services being traded in a regulated environment.

" Internet companies that specialise in sales to business have greater potential than those that sell to customers. **"**

❖ The Big Ideas

☐ Business Applications

Most commentators believe that 'the business-to-business' sector is the 'next big thing' in e-commerce. Provision of services to small, medium and large businesses over the Internet promises to improve their efficiency and profitability.

They will, for instance be able to use the Internet to compare prices to save on desktop supplies and equipment, save on freight, streamline an import business and track deliveries. Here is just a sample of possible services:

Executive

- the development of business plans
- communication with trading partners
- identification of performance of product lines

Finance

- financial planning
- expense reports
- purchase requests
- e-procurement
- invoicing
- payment
- banking
- quotes

Manufacturing

- supply chain management
- logistics
- inventory control
- predict order completion date

Human Resources

- recruitment
- salary survey services
- employee background checks
- employee records

Sales

- customer relationship management (CRM)
- contact management
- market research
- identification of best geographic areas for sales

Most businesses will already have computer programs in place to perform some or all of these functions. Many larger to medium sized companies spent a lot of money upgrading their management systems in the period preceding Y2K. However, many of these systems tend to be focussed on the internal functions of a company rather than outwardly. In the world of e-commerce developing efficient communication and cooperation with suppliers and customers will be vital. All industry categories are likely to benefit, at least somewhat, by adopting an e-commerce approach but experts believe that there could be especially widespread interest in the electronics, chemical, computer hardware and software suppliers, automobile manufacturers and parts suppliers, medicine and transportation sectors.

> **"** A seamless supply chain is an essential ingredient to successful e-commerce. **"**

☐ Do you choose your Service from a 'Shopping Mall' or Lease On-Line?

To date most large and medium companies have bought integrated business application packages from one of five Application Service Providers (ASPs); JD Edwards, Baan, Oracle, PeopleSoft and SAP. Large companies may have spent as much as $100 million on adoption and implementation. However, these suppliers of software are facing a challenge. Some customers are not entirely happy with the product. Because the systems integrate many business functions they tend to be cumbersome. Only a small percentage of people in a business use them and they are often not good at retrieving old data. The products will also need to be modified somewhat to incorporate e-commerce into their functions and provide access to some of the data base not only to managers but also most other employees in the company and possibly customers.

> **"** People have suddenly realised the profits that can be made from on-line small-business centres. **"**

All this has led to the emergence of two other approaches to purchasing business support services. The first involves software companies like those listed above leasing their product rather than selling it outright to a business and providing access to it remotely over the Internet. The advantage to a business using the product is that they commit less up front money to a product and can take advantage of software upgrades. The advantage to the software companies is that they capture customers who they can serve and keep loyal by offering special individualised services.

The second alternative involves the development of small business web sites that are Internet portals specialising in providing services to one or more business sectors. These portals gather together a wide range of business-related service companies. This allows businesses to choose the 'best of breed' supplier for each of the services required, rather than rely on one service provider to supply an integrated package. Such business web sites attract companies to visit their portal with free products like downloadable business letters and free information like access to legal material and listings of upcoming trade shows. The advantage to businesses is that they are likely to get better prices by shopping around for services and supplies.

❑ The Advent of Aggregators, Auctions and Exchanges as Avenues for Buying and Selling Goods and Services

The Internet has spawned a number of other ways of undertaking business-to-business transactions. Aggregators, for instance, are a new breed of businesses that use the Internet to offer customers the best possible prices. They do this by convincing what hitherto had been rival companies to combine their buying power to purchase supplies in bulk. At the same time they draw together rival suppliers to offer a large pool of product for a business sector at pre-determined prices. Auctions (see also 'e-sales') allow businesses to offload their surplus product in a market where buyers compete for bargains. Exchanges (following the example of stock exchanges) provide businesses with the opportunity to trade product and services in a stable, regulated on-line market with vetted participants, clear rules and freely available trading information.

Two Examples of Initiatives

❑ Overcoming the 'Tyranny of Distance': A Regional Initiative

The Internet site, Heartland, provides a service to the Central Economic Zone of New South Wales, consisting of 300 000 people and 20 000 businesses. It is designed to help businesses in the region overcome the 'tyranny of distance' by giving them help to develop an on-line trading presence on the Internet. The site also provides tourist information, local weather and services to farmers.

☐ Industry-Specific Trading Networks

Industry-specific trading networks bring together wholesale suppliers, vendors and retailers and offer integrated logistical support to help companies cut costs in specific industries. For instance, the Australian government and the pharmaceutical industry have joined forces to develop the Pharmaceutical Extranet Gateway, an electronic ordering system for manufacturers, suppliers and customers. The system promises order-processing accuracy, advanced delivery notifications, shared business information and streamlined payments. One report indicated that the industry expected the cost of placing an order could decrease from $75 to $5 by implementation of the system.

THE WORLD AND AUSTRALIAN ECONOMIES

☆ Main Point

Signs are good that worldwide economic growth, enhanced by widespread adoption of business-to-business e-commerce, will be sustained over the first few years of the twenty-first century.

✓ Executive Summary

Many economists suggest that the business environment that exists at the start of the twenty-first century has the potential to bring sustained worldwide economic growth. This optimism is based on a unique combination of developments. Globalisation has seen the internationalisation of trade, investment, ownership and services. New markets are available to outward-looking entrepreneurs. Business-to-business e-commerce is set to boom over the next few years, speeding up transactions and bringing large savings in the supply and distribution of goods. With the advent of the Internet, obstacles to growth such as location and size become less important than the ability to provide excellent service. Service becomes as important as the provision of quality goods. Australia should flourish in this economic environment. Its economy is in good shape. It has a flexible, relatively cheap and well-trained workforce that has considerable expertise in the provision of service. It has a well-developed telecommunications infrastructure and has experience trading in world markets. The biggest threat to continued worldwide growth could come from a meltdown in over-priced US Internet shares. This, however, seems less and less likely as investors have already begun to flee from the more speculative end of the market.

> 66 ...if the big problem since the early '70s has been finding jobs for people, the big problem of the new decade will be finding people for jobs. 99
>
> John Edwards, The Australian Financial Review, 30-31/10/99.

❖ The Big Ideas

❏ Why the World Economy is Strong

Dr David Clark, from the School of Economics, University of New South Wales, speaking at the Brisbane Club in September

1999, suggested that the twenty-first century would be the most dynamic era in the history of capitalism. These are a number of contributing factors that have brought us to this point. From 1850 until 1930 a reduction in the costs for transportation meant that international trade expanded exponentially. Then, in 1990, the costs of communication began to drop. Lastly, starting in about 1989, came the information technology revolution. It did not have the initial impact that it could have had because its influence on trade was masked by the sudden downturn in the Asian economies. However, the crises in Asia seem to be behind us, heralding a period of rapid worldwide economic growth for the beginning of the twenty-first century.

A lot now depends on the economic health of the US. Its economy is strong for a number of reasons. It dominates worldwide IT industries. Deregulation, tax cuts, a balanced budget and low inflation have helped nurture economic growth. Productivity has continued to rise and with freer international trade, the Western Hemisphere has seen steady growth. The general health of the global economy is such that it survived crises such as the Japanese banking crisis in the early 90s, the Mexican crisis of 1995 and the 1997-1998 Asian crisis. This is partly because businesses have become flexible enough to be able to find markets elsewhere if there is a downturn in demand from a traditional customer.

☐ The Economic Future for the World and Australia

There are indications that the major economies in the world will continue to grow as businesses, large and small, incorporate business-to-business e-commerce in their corporate plans, increase efficiency in supply line logistics and decrease costs. Perhaps the biggest danger to continued economic growth is the devastating crash in over-priced US Internet stocks. Some US commentators are suggesting that up to 90% of recently listed US Internet businesses have no chance of ever making a profit and will implode sooner rather than later. If this happens, we could possibly see the plunge in the US stockmarket precipitating a worldwide recession. However, this seems less likely to happen as US investors are recognising that many upstarts have only 'blue sky' to recommend them and are reducing their exposure to the speculative end of the

" (Australia has) a small, wealthy economy with a big service sector, a well-trained, highly skilled, English-speaking but multicultural and relatively cheap workforce, which also offers a natural and built environment that is better than most. **"**

John Edwards, The Australian Financial Review, 30-31/10/99.

" The act of saving has practically died for many people in North America, the UK and Australia. **"**

IT market. Many of these companies are now listing at prices below their initial offering price. Their final demise should be no surprise.

Economically, Australia is in good shape. By the end of the 90s Australia had experienced the longest period of economic expansion for over 50 years. Commentators suggest that this expansion is due to a combination of four factors. During the 90s Australia saw a rapid growth in productivity, much faster than in many comparable developed nations. Growth was much better in the service industries than in the production of physical goods. This has been attributed to the ready availability of inexpensive computers and telecommunications together with a reform of work practices and the development of a flexible and well-trained work force. Nations with lower labour costs, especially those in China and South East Asia, have taken over the task of manufacturing goods cheaply. The second factor was a lengthy period of low inflation. The third factor is a reduction in dependence on mining, manufacturing and primary industries and the expansion of telecommunications and financial service industries. The last factor has been increasing globalisation. Because of its small domestic market and isolation Australia has always been open to international trade. With the opening of worldwide markets Australia has, in some areas, been quick to exploit opportunities. In a global market environment, Australia is likely to benefit because of its continued high investment in information technology and telecommunications. Business-to business e-commerce is set to boom and manufacturers should be able to expand their export drive. In some areas of technology, Australia lags up to two years behind the US. This puts Australia at a disadvantage in that it is unable to compete to gain 'first strike advantage' in some markets. On the other hand it can benefit by learning from and not making the same mistakes as US companies that are first in the field. In other areas, such as mobile phone development, Australia (and Europe) leads the US, which has not yet decided on common formats for its networks.

Australia faces a strange economic situation. Australian government debt has been reduced substantially through tight fiscal policy. However, at the same time, a wealth dichotomy has arisen within the community. The rich continue to become wealthier while many in the rest of the nation have used up their savings and borrow to maintain their lifestyle. This is particularly marked for low-income earners and the aged. Lots of jobs will be available for skilled workers this decade. Shortages could occur in some industries if plans are not put in place to train specialists in fields such as e-commerce, tourism, financial services, business services and telecommunications.

Reference

Edwards,J.(1999). Australia's Economic Revolution. Sydney, UNSW Press.

CHANGES IN BANKING: BANKING ON CHANGE

☆ Main Point

Technology has revolutionised banking and banks continue to exploit opportunities made possible by the Internet. This promises to continue to increase the profitability of banks. Customers, too, should benefit from a broader range of services that are both cheaper and more accessible than ever before.

✓ Executive Summary

Banks have become profitable because of their ability to see ways technology could add value to their business. Although the adoption of new technologies has increased efficiency it has been at the cost of traditional jobs in the industry. However, new jobs will emerge with the adoption of the Internet by banks as the main avenue for doing business.

Banks see a rosy future as key players in the Internet economy. Two major areas are likely to be exploited: business to business transactions and the use of portals to the Internet. Banks have the enviable advantage of having a well established reputation for trustworthiness and a large cohort of, often, loyal customers. Although in its infancy, Internet banking can offer customers a broad range of services that are cheaper and more accessible than in the past.

Speed is of the essence if banks wish to establish a major presence on the Internet and a competitive advantage. Typically they are doing this by forming alliances with other businesses that can help them quickly reach their goals. For instance, mobile phone banking and cashless transactions loom as major features of banking.

❖ The Big Ideas

☐ Taking Advantage of Technology

Over the past few years banks in Australia have seen a substantial increase in profitability. This has come about by their using technology to be more efficient and, at the same time,

> **"** ....cost reduction (by banks) has, to an important extent, been due to the introduction of new technologies which have enabled banks to reduce the number of staff, and the size and number of branches. **"**
>
> Reserve Bank, June Report, quoted by Dan Coyne, The Australian Financial Review, 20/9/99.

enabling them to cut labour costs. Automatic Teller Machines (ATMs), Electronic Funds Transfer at Point of Sale (EFTPOS) and phone banking are all considerably cheaper than dealing with a teller. The current estimated costs per transaction are: for dealing with a teller $2-1.30; phone banking 75 cents; using an ATM 80-45 cents and EFTPOS 40 cents. It is estimated that nearly 40% of bank customers use phone banking, two thirds use EFTPOS transactions and 70% use ATMs.

However, banking is still in transition. ATMs are in for a re-vamp. Relatively soon customers will be able to conduct a much wider range of banking functions at ATMs. Before this can happen, the older machines (those with narrow slits to look through) will need to be replaced. Some of the most modern ATMs are now capable of customer recognition using iris scanning. Web-enabled ATMs will eventually dominate the market. Some customers have a direct line from their PCs to their bank and Internet banking is slowly increasing in popularity. The costs of these services are 35 cents and 21 cents respectively. We can expect greater use of the Internet for banking once customers are convinced that security and privacy are not problems.

☐ Exploiting the Possibilities of the Internet

Banks can now see a very rosy future as part of the expected explosion of e-commerce. Established banks should blossom in an e-commerce world for a number of reasons. They already have a large client base, many of which are loyal customers. Established banks have a reputation for honesty and reliability; both important attributes in the e-world, where trustworthiness is an important commodity. Banks also already have an established electronic infrastructure. They are therefore in a position to exploit the two major growth areas of the Internet: business-to-business transactions (B2B) and the establishment of portals to the Internet for shopping and every other conceivable transaction. For example, the National Australia Bank (NAB) has entered into an alliance with ISP Freeonline and offers its banking customers 150 minutes a day free Internet access.

> **"** E-commerce will fundamentally change the way we do business and banks are leading the revolution. **"**

☐ Good Allies and Speed the Key Ingredients to Gaining a Competitive Edge

❝ Slow off the mark, big businesses are forming alliances and working at light speed to catch up to upstart companies that have led the way exploiting the possibilities of the net. **❞**

Banks are rapidly spreading into new markets. The Commonwealth Bank (CBA) has very quickly established an offshoot discount sharebroking arm, Commonwealth Securities, that has become the biggest on-line broking firm in terms of volume of transactions and the second most visited Web site in Australia after ninemsn. CBA has also entered into a wide range of alliances both domestically and internationally to exploit e-commerce opportunities. On the domestic front, CBA bought part of EDS Australia which, in turn will supply IT services to the bank. CBA has formed an alliance with Woolworths and McDonalds to offer customers in-store banking facilities. Other banks have opened banking outlets in Coles-Myer stores. The CBA has entered into an agreement with Vodafone to exploit banking by mobile phone. CBA now plans to form alliances overseas to exploit opportunities in e-commerce leading eventually to it being a global force in financial services.

☐ Internet Banking

❝ If you want customers to return to your financial services site make it simple and user friendly. **❞**

Over the past few years, the United States has seen the phenomenon of 'Internet-only' banks spring up. Because they have little investment in bricks and mortar, they can offer lower bank charges than regular banks. In Australia, as time goes on, we may well see a blurring of the distinctions between banks, finance companies, insurance companies, broking, financial advisers and the like. Many of the large banks or their customers have been relatively slow to recognise the advantages of Internet banking. In the e-world, providing added value is a key to maintaining customer loyalty and attracting new customers. Some of the options banks can offer customers through the Internet are:

- A low cost 24-hour service.
- Access to an account from any PC anywhere.
- Payment to accounts of individuals and businesses situated at other banks.
- Access to a wide range of other resources such as loan applications
- Secure payroll management for small businesses
- End-of-year financial statements
- Shopping on-line.

Only two percent of Australians use Internet banking but that has increased by 300% in the last year. The banks, in order of number of on-line transactions in September 1999, were estimated to be: CBA, NAB, Australia New Zealand Bank (ANZ), Westpac and St George.

Banks will all soon offer mobile phone banking. The most advanced technology for the purpose is called Wireless Application Protocol (WAP). Customers will need to own a wide-screen format mobile phone that can display static and moving images. These are similar to, but simpler than, those found on an Internet page. The service allows customers to determine account balances and request statements as well as making transactions. The system would also allow banks to alert customers when their credit card balance was reaching its overdraft limit. Share trading using a mobile phone is also planned for the future.

☐ Cashless Transactions

Over the next few years, as security and privacy concerns are allayed, we will move towards a cashless society, based on credit and direct debit from accounts with the ability for bank customers to either be alerted about each transaction or be able to check balances on command.

> **"** ....security and privacy rank as two of the more serious impediments to any wholesale acceptance of Internet banking. **"**
>
> Dan Coyne, The Australian Financial Review, 20/9/99.

STOCKBROKERS FACE AN INDUSTRIAL REVOLUTION

☆ Main Point

The Internet has had a massive influence on stockbroking with increasing numbers of traders making transactions on-line because of the speed and ease of transaction and low transaction costs. In response to this threat to their livelihood brokers have chosen to specialise, transition into financial advising or offer a premium service to wealthy customers. On-line services that prosper will offer a reliable service that is seen as good value for money.

☐ Executive Summary

In many ways the Internet is ideal for trading in company shares. It is a fast form of communication. In its most elemental form, the sending of a brief message to an on-line stockbroking firm, it is inexpensive. The Internet can also provide the customer with ready access to a plethora of information including information about latest floats, the health of companies and the current value of a personal portfolio. Plotting of trends and in-depth analysis are also easy to provide. So it is no wonder that on-line trading has seen such a successful introduction in Australia.

However, on-line trading has meant that traditional brokers have had to decide whether they can afford to remain the same or adopt a new role. Some will still provide a high quality service for the rich and institutional clients. But most will choose other avenues including setting up an on-line presence.

Traditional stock exchanges have also had to review their role. Some face challenges from alternative trading systems. They also realise that they need to develop greater international ties as the globalisation of financial markets increases in pace. Extended trading hours, even 24-hour trading may be necessary in some bourses.

❖ The Big Ideas

❑ Some Statistics

- The transactions made by large institutions still dominate the number of shares traded and, ultimately what happens to the stock market.
- Over thirty percent of Australians now own shares in Australian companies.
- At the start of 2000 over 10 percent of transactions on the Australian Stock Exchange were on the Internet.
- At the start of 2000 the majority of Australia's major retail banks started their own on-line discount broking services.
- On-line brokers can charge much less than the broking fee of full service brokers.
- Commonwealth Securities, the biggest trader by volume, has over 60 000 on-line customers of which a third log on to the site daily.
- By 2003 it has been predicted that Australia will have the third largest amount of funds under investment (after the US and Switzerland).

❝ Electronic trading is to the financial markets as the jet engine was to international travel. **❞**

❑ The Future of Broking

The advent of on-line trading has sent shock waves through the stock broking industry. Faced with competition from on-line services that process stock transactions at a fraction of the regular price, brokers have had to review the way they do business. It is likely that many former stockbrokers will choose to specialise in one of the functions that are a sub-set of broking. These include the execution of orders, research and advice, management of funds and clearing and settlements. One stockbroking firm has made its efficient settlement system available to other brokers converting what had been a liability into one that makes a profit. Other stockbrokers will offer full services to customers. These customers (often institutional or wealthy) will tend to remain loyal to their stockbrokers because the higher broking fees bring compensations such as quality research, analysis, advice and access to new share issues. There will also be companies that provide 'one-stop-shopping' including banking, broking, superannuation services and investment advice.

❝ The discount firms are working on fine margins and the agency firms are under pressure. **❞**

Trevor Sykes, The Australian Financial Review, 11-12/9/99.

☐ On-Line Broking

" The internet is an ideal medium for share trading. It has never been easier to maintain your portfolio. **"**

However, the most common type of broker in the future is likely to be one that offers an easy to use, on-line service with very competitive transaction rates combined with immediate access to up-to-date information but no advice. Since competition between on-line brokers will be fierce we will see them adding value with a variety of extras such as margin lending, a discount managed funds service, access to international shares, free charts, monitoring of portfolios and 'stock watch lists'. Many more services could be added, such as market commentaries, company profiles, graphing tools, notification of floats and paging when a 'sell price' is reached. Access to a large client base (something the major banks already have) will be a key to success in on-line banking because it is the volume of transactions that is most important. There will still be a place for financial advisers because of the sheer volume of information available to investors and their need of help to see 'the big picture' and make sound decisions. However, above everything else, continuous and reliable service will be a key to customer loyalty. Customers are not likely to be patient with an on-line service that has one too many glitches.

" On-line stockbroking has enabled more people than ever before to play the stockmarket. **"**

☐ Stock Exchanges

Stock exchanges are also facing competition. In the United States traditional stock exchanges are not only facing a challenge from upstart exchanges, but also from companies that match 'buy' and 'sell' orders from clients, through alternative trading systems called electronic communications networks (ECNs). The Australian Stock Exchange (ASX) is now facing competition from Computershare which has hitherto earned much of its income by acting as a share registry and selling financial market software to foreign stock exchanges. There are reports that Computershare plans to compete with the ASX in exchange services. All this has combined to make the business of enabling the trading of shares a very competitive and stressful business.

In the meantime opportunities are increasing for investors to participate in trade overseas. Clients are now able to trade in shares on many of the world's stock exchanges including those in the United States, Britain and Japan. This may mean extended trading in exchanges around the world. In small markets such as those in Australia extended trading may affect the liquidity of stock. International stock trading might eventually result in some sort of amalgamation of world stock exchanges. However, most commentators suggest that the possibility of a world stock exchange is many years away.

> " Stock exchanges have changed dramatically. They have extended their hours, can match orders electronically, incorporate on-line trading and link so easily to other bourses around the world that there is the potential for a global exchange. "

CALL CENTRES & CUSTOMER RELATIONSHIP MANAGEMENT

☆ Main Point

Call centres have mushroomed to meet the growing demands of an increasingly sophisticated consumer market. Good service is being recognised as a key business characteristic and Customer Relationship Management (CRM) is seen as a critical element in doing business.

✓ Executive Summary

Call centres deal with customer service or support marketing and have become one of the fastest growing business components worldwide. Nearly one percent of Australians work in call centres and, by the year 2002 two percent of people in the United Kingdom will work in call centres. This growth has come about because of the realisation that customer-service matters in a market that is increasingly sophisticated and fickle.

As call centres have become increasingly sophisticated, so too are the demands on the agents that work in them. Turn over of agents is high and this continues to be a drain on businesses. The costs of training staff could be reduced, however, by out-sourcing the call centre function to a private company. One of the advantages of call centres is that they can be situated anywhere. This can be a boon to rural Australia. Australia is also strategically placed to take advantage of call centre traffic from North America and Europe.

Customer Relationship Management (CRM) is that set of practices designed to develop and maintain lifetime customer loyalty. This is achieved in a number of ways. Knowing who the customer is and what the customer wants means that the business can serve the customer better. Gathering this sort of information can be part of the role of call centres. CRM can also serve to keep the customer happy with special treatment for good customers.

❖ The Big Ideas

❑ Call Centres

Call centres consist of a group of workers using electronic communication (often phones but increasingly using the Internet) who communicate with customers. This can take two main forms. Some call centres serve the public by providing information. A simple call centre might be called a help desk or a sales and service desk. The main objective of a second type of call centre is to sell products or gain information about potential buyers. The tasks involved in such call centres might be telemarketing or tele-sales. A sophisticated consumer market, demanding high levels of service using the latest technology, has increased competition amongst service providers resulting in a phenomenal growth in call centres.

Call centres have created a new demand in the labour market. The skills required of operators in these centres (commonly referred to as 'agents') have become more sophisticated as the value of call centres has increased. Agents are now a critical part of Customer Relationship Management (CRM), a function that is profit-driven and vital to business growth and retention of customers. Although call centre agents have traditionally been poorly paid, this is changing as their value to the business is increasing and their skills become increasingly in demand. Executive positions in call centre management are becoming more integral to businesses and can command salaries in excess of $250,000.

With increasing sophistication of service, call centre agents are often required to use knowledge systems and databases and have an understanding of business processes. Training for agents is typically for an eight-week period and can cost as much as $11 000. Unfortunately, turn-over of agents is high (as much as 25% per annum) resulting in annual turn-over costs to the industry of $100 million.

Call centres can be located anywhere. They do not need to be close to head office. They do not even have to be in the same country as the organisation they represent. Australia is in a prime position to take advantage of the call centre market. Situated in the economically important Asian time zone, it is distant from the time zones of both North America and

" Call centres are proliferating so rapidly it is becoming difficult to find staff. **"**

Europe. Australian call centres also employ a large number of well trained, multi-lingual, multi-skilled and articulate people. So Australia is attractive because it can provide call centres that are highly professional. However, it faces the threat of competition from call centres in countries with large populations and lower labour rates. With call centre technology making geographic location irrelevant, call centres can easily be set up in Australian country areas where they can provide regional employment. Because labour is often cheaper in the country and two thirds of a call centre's cost is labour, it makes good economic sense to set up centres there.

☐ CRM: Customer Relationship Management

A key management focus these days is Customer Relationship Management (CRM). It promises improved effectiveness of communication between company and customer resulting in increased customer satisfaction and loyalty.

CRM is about retaining customers, providing lifetime value to customers and maximising new business opportunities and profitability. Effective CRM strategy has a multi-channel focus using Internet, call centre software and self-service websites, kiosks and email. As business moves to more holistic performance measures which include customer satisfaction, call centres are providing a broader role in managing the customer relationships.

Businesses are now seeing the value of using customer data, harvested in call centres for sales, for marketing, developing business and competitive advantage. For instance, data gathered through call centres can now be used to improve service or add or delete product offerings. This practice is not looked on favourably by civil libertarians who see it as a further invasion of privacy.

Businesses are also able to offer selective service. It works like this. Let us say that you are a valued customer of a company. When you make a call to the centre your phone number is automatically 'recognised' as a 'valued customer' and your call is moved to the head of the queue or shunted to a special customer service representative. On the other hand, if your phone number is 'recognised' as that of a chronic nuisance or complainer you may find that you wait a long time in the queue. Of course, you never get to know that this is being done!

Some companies, faced with the complexities of managing a burgeoning call centre, may decide to outsource it to an independent operator. The risk is that they also outsource their corporate image and reputation. The growth of call centres as value-added profit centres may therefore convince management to keep profit and competitive customer information inside the parent organisation.

☐ Statistics of Future Growth

The call centre market still is seen as immature and strong growth is expected.

- ACA Research estimates that the Australian call centre industry is valued at $6.5 billion, employing 160,000 people in 4,000 call centres across Australia and is growing at the rate of 25 percent each year. (Australian Financial Review 23/11/99)

- ACA Research predicts that in the Asia-Pacific Region, in the next two years, the value of customer relationship management will increase ten times, from around $300 million to $3 billion.

JOBS

☆ Main Point

The advent of the Internet and the rise of economic rationalism have combined to create a 'change-responsive business culture' which, in turn, has resulted in a new worker demographic: skilled, flexible, efficient, 'on contract' and 'on the move'.

✓ Executive Summary

The Internet has changed the way many of us will work (see The Internet Revolution; Stockbroking; Selling on the Internet; A Revolution in Education). For instance, many car sales people and university lecturers will find some of their functions replaced by Internet web sites. But other jobs will appear. These will include jobs that can migrate from the old world to the net (eg., journalism), jobs that provide web maintenance (eg., web masters) and jobs that are offshoots of Internet activity (eg., courier services).

Economic rationalism and a 'change-responsive culture' have resulted in businesses endeavouring to become leaner, more efficient and more flexible in the face of massive changes around them. This has led to the replacement of permanent staff (downsizing) by part-timers and a burgeoning service community (outsourcing). This, in turn, has affected how much work people do, where they do it and when. Lack of job security has become a big issue.

Jobs are also likely to be affected by three different trends. The first, the ageing of the baby boomer generation promises to support a growth in tourism, entertainment and eventually the health-care industries. At the same time, the growth of cheap alternative labour markets and robotics promise to reduce opportunities for employment in the manufacturing industries in developed nations like Australia. Globalisation has also meant that labour markets are slowly opening up with talent flowing both into and out of Australia depending on demand and salary differentials.

❖ The Big Ideas

☐ Effects of Economic Rationalism

Economic rationalism has meant that many companies have chosen to employ fewer people, pay them more, work them harder and replace them if they falter. In the elite professions like law, medicine and senior management long hours are expected and stress and fatigue are worn as badges of honour. Yet the results of such practices can be bad for both the individual and society. Stress in the individual can result in chronic fatigue, heart attacks, depression, absenteeism and family breakdown. A stressed individual is more likely to give poor service to clients. Nobody wins. Realising this, some enlightened companies have introduced 'family-friendly work practices', offering flexible work opportunities such as permanent part-time work and provision of child care facilities. The pay-off is that the workforce is more relaxed and contented and more committed. Talent is retained. The company benefits from higher quality output of employees and a reduced cost for hiring and training new staff.

> **"** Being expected to work longer, harder and faster, under the constant threat of dismissal for failure, means workers are stressed and their health is suffering. **"**

Many companies have been able to increase productivity and the bottom line by reducing their work to a main function and out-sourcing many other functions considered not to be core business. These include cleaning, information technology, legal services, payroll, marketing, human resources and even prime manufacturing. This trend has had two other results. Workers retained by a company can find that they have to perform additional tasks inherited from sacked colleagues. Sacked colleagues can, in the meantime, be picked up by outside agencies that offer out-sourcing services to business and industry. At the same time the demand for top talent in management and information technology has never been greater. While some top IT talent is leaving for plum jobs in the US there are cases of the work they leave behind being out-sourced to workers in India. With such a mobile workforce, loyalty to a company diminishes. Companies find that, to retain key staff, they need to offer incentives such as share options, support for further study and inclusion in succession planning.

☐ Outsourcing

" I often work seven days a week for weeks on end trying to meet a deadline. I typically get four or five hours sleep but, on occasion I've worked fifty hours straight. **"**

Service to business is the third biggest industry in Australia behind manufacturing and wholesaling. By the year 2003 it should employ about one million people, many part-time, in six main service areas; computing, law and accounting, management, marketing, technical support and scientific research. Computing includes data processing, databases and computer maintenance. Marketing includes advertising, graphic design and market research. Other services include recruitment and security.

Businesses have found that there is something of an art to out-sourcing. The key to a successful out-sourcing agreement is clear, open communication. The provider needs to understand the requirements and goals of the client. The client needs to make an accurate estimation of the capabilities of the provider. It is essential, for instance, that the provider understands the business and the level of service required.

Businesses have out-sourced functions because out-sourcing firms pay their own employees less, so that they can charge the client less than it would cost for the client to employ their own workers to perform the same function. However, a recent legal ruling has indicated that, when a business out-sources functions, existing awards and agreements still apply to the work done. If the work performed by an employee of an outsource agency is the same as the work that would have been performed in-house for a client, the salary must be the same. This ruling would seem to indicate that companies will be unable to cut costs by out-sourcing.

" ...about 30 per cent of (Australian) full-time workers now work more than 49 hours a week...... while only about one third of the workforce works standard hours. **"**

Annabel Hepworth, The Australian Financial Review, 17/9/99.

Not only does big business outsource certain functions but we are finding that DINTs (double income- no time) and DINKs (double income- no kids) are also doing so. Why not have your house cleaned, lawn mowed, your clothes ironed, your car washed and your food prepared by someone else, if you can afford it? And many couples, where both partners work, can afford these services. Those who perform these domestic functions are likely to find full employment but a relatively poor income.

❑ Telecommuting

Telecommuters work at home but are employed by a corporation. Of the 300 000 telecommuters identified in an Australian Bureau of Statistics study in 1998, seventy per cent were males and the majority were between the ages of 25 and 39.

There are those who enjoy the flexibility of working at home. An avid golfer could, for instance, play a game in the morning and make up the time by working late at night. However, there can be problems associated with working at home. Some may miss the human contact provided in an office setting. A telecommuter might be expected, by a spouse, to perform 'home tasks' like running errands as well as working full-time from home. Home workers do not have the advantage of an in-house computer technician when a computer misbehaves. There is also more likelihood of mis-communication with a client or boss via phone and e-mail than there would be if communication were face-to-face. The largest segment of the work force working out of home come from the information technology field.

❑ Permanent Part-time, Part-time, Casual or Unemployed

Because employers want to remain flexible, they are out-sourcing more functions. This has already had a profound effect on the shape of employment. A quarter of Australia's 8.8 million workers are now part-timers. Traditionally, women have dominated part-time and casual positions. But recent reports indicate that more men are finding part-time work. The 'job-for-life' of twenty years ago has been replaced by an employment mode that is much more fluid. Many more people will be in a form of employment that is not permanent full-time. A common mode of employment will be a short-term contract lasting months. This will suit some. Those with marketable skills will be happy not to be tied to one job too long. They have ambitions and see a series of jobs helping them build a portfolio of experiences that makes them more marketable for the next one. Because more workers will be 'free-agents' there will be a need for all but the very best to 'sell themselves' for the next contract. Another employment mode will see permanent employees working on a part-time basis.

" By 2005 more than half of all workers under 25 and half of those over 45 are likely to be in part-time work rather than full-time. "

This may often be for lifestyle reasons or because they wish to work on two or more jobs. However, part-time employment brings with it a sense of insecurity, of impermanence. The best many of us can hope for is to have a series of interesting and fulfilling jobs (or even a series of different careers) in our work-life.

☐ Hot-Desking

Hot-desking involves a number of employees in an organisation, often with the same roles, sharing the same desk in the office. The practice allows an employer to cut costs on furniture and equipment where a number of employees use a desk only occasionally in their work. Sales people, for instance, often work away from a desk. Workers in call centres seldom have their own desks but are assigned a vacant one each shift. However, it is not popular with staff who would prefer to have their own work-stations.

☐ Hot Jobs

Hot jobs will increasingly be advertised on the Internet. The process is reasonably inexpensive, fast and reaches a global audience. The Internet even makes possible a situation where an employee does not even have to live in the same country as the employer. An example of this phenomenon was recently reported in the Australian Financial Review. Two researchers at a university in Australia were offered lucrative appointments by an American company. They liked the offer but they didn't want to uproot their families to move to the US. No problem. The American company suggested they set up an office in Australia and conduct their business over the Internet. They now have the jobs they wanted and can still enjoy the Australian lifestyle.

The information technology (IT) industry is expanding exponentially. In the US, which is a little ahead of Australia, the Commerce Department has projected that, by 2006, nearly half of their workforce will be in IT industries. Universities cannot keep pace with the demand for IT graduates and suitable candidates for jobs are being sourced from overseas. Some pundits are suggesting that, in Australia, the shortage could rise to 200 000 jobs over the next few years. With computer chips in everything from cars to refrigerators the demand for people to service machines is also likely to increase.

The service industry will become one of the largest in the nation over the next few years. Large accounting firms, placement agencies and law firms have extended the range of the services they offer, to meet the out-sourcing needs of big business. At the other end of the scale, small businesses are meeting the out-sourcing needs of busy couples with a wide range of services. The baby boomers will also provide opportunities in a number of areas (see Baby Boomers). Because of their comparative affluence and time on their hands, retired baby boomers are expected to boost the recreation, travel and entertainment industries and, in time, aged care. The out-sourcing industry will be highly competitive. Owner-operators will need good management skills and the services provided will need to be efficient, effective, competitively priced and will need to be seen to add value.

☐ Recruitment on-line

On-line recruitment is becoming big business. Depending on which source you believe there are between 70 and 200 on-line recruitment sites in Australia. The Recruitment and Consulting Services Association of Australia has estimated that recruitment advertising will amount to $450 million during 2000 and recruitment agencies will earn $3.5 billion in placement fees. (Australian Financial Review 05/11/99). There are predictions that, within the next year, on-line recruitment will become the choice for job hunting and placement.

The trend is emerging where IT and many professional jobs are now advertised on-line. The trend is for most IT jobs and many professional jobs to be recruited on-line. Job seekers have access to more jobs on-line than there are in newspapers. Job applicants will soon be in a position to submit CV's on-line and , in some cases, be notified immediately whether a match occurs. Applicants are still to be convinced, however, that there is guaranteed security (hence confidentiality) when posting to an on-line service.

Although many companies are using web sites for recruitment the practice is not without its drawbacks. Some companies are becoming swamped by so many applications hitting the in-box.

Many responses come from overseas applicants who do not have current visa status. So companies need to decide whether they want to do their own recruiting or use a recruitment firm.

On-line recruitment companies operate in a highly competitive market. They need to advertise in the print or other media to attract people to their site. Sites need to be up to date and need to maintain a fresh look if they are to keep customers. Service will be the key differentiator. Added value might include backing the site with a call centre open between 8 am and midnight, seven days a week. Some agencies notify registered applicants of matching jobs and offer on-line aptitude tests. Clearly markets will shake out and mergers and alliances will lead to a few large agencies dominating the market.

While everyone agrees that on-line recruitment is growing, there is ongoing debate about the impact this will have on newspapers. It would seem clear that an expansion of on-line recruitment would result in a corresponding decrease in advertising in the print media. However, the future is not too gloomy for newspapers. The biggest advertisers in Australia are governments and they (for equity reasons) are obliged to make their ads available in the print media. Secondly, on-line agencies, needing the exposure, have taken to advertising their sites in newspapers. Lastly, to cover their bets, print media companies are getting into the on-line recruitment market as well.

☐ Work and Gender

The Australian Bureau of Statistics has reported that the per cent of females in work has risen from 44.6 per cent of women in 1983 to 54.4 per cent of women in 1999, while male participation rates have fallen from 77.1 percent to 72.6 percent. More women than men are in casual or part-time work. Their numbers are likely to grow, as mining and manufacturing are replaced by service industries, call centres, hospitality and leisure. However, at the other end of the scale, there are only 8 per cent of women as directors on Australia's company boards.

☐ Work and Disabilities

The Internet should prove to be a boon for the disabled who will now be able to perform tasks away from the traditional workplace. They no longer need be disadvantaged by problems with transportation or with access to buildings.

Part Two:

Government

GLOBAL WARMING, KYOTO & THE ENVIRONMENT

☆ Main Point

The surface of the earth is warming and the burning of fossil fuels is likely to have contributed. Governments have agreed to reduce burning but there are doubts about whether this will significantly reduce greenhouse gas emissions. Meanwhile people continue to degrade the environment.

✓ Executive Summary

There is general agreement amongst most scientists that the surface of the earth has warmed over the past one hundred years. What is less clear is the magnitude of the warming trend and the extent of the contribution to surface warming that can be attributed to greenhouse gases.

At a meeting of government representatives in Kyoto it was agreed that developed nations need to reduce emission of greenhouse gases by certain deadlines. Australia is in an unenviable position because it is a major exporter and user of carbon (fossil) fuels. The imposition of a carbon tax by governments is one scheme proposed for convincing industry to reduce its fuel consumption. These taxes would need to be so high that it could force closure of mines and industries. A second plan involving the buying of 'carbon credits' by fuel producers and users from tree farms is likely to only offset about three percent of Australia's greenhouse gas emissions. So it is problematic whether Australia will be able to meet its commitments to reducing greenhouse gas emissions by the deadline of 2008. In the meantime the US has said it will only follow the Kyoto Protocol if developing nations are required to also reduce emissions.

Australia could reduce carbon gas emissions if it used nuclear power stations and required major changes to car manufacture, neither of which is likely for politically reasons. Solar energy, wind power and hot rock energy schemes are being tried but do not offer short-term solutions to the problem. Meanwhile Australia faces other environmental problems with salt in rising water tables threatening to contaminate rural land.

Industrial chemicals are killing or incapacitating workers. Wildlife, worldwide is being decimated.

❖ The Big Ideas

◻ Global Warming

❝ Surface temperatures in the past two decades have risen at a rate substantially greater than average for the past 100 years. **❞**

National Research Council of the (US) National Academies report, 12/1/00.

Major studies by scientists agree that worldwide data suggests the temperature of the surface of the earth has increased over the past century (National Research Council of the National Academies, 2000; Jones & Wigley, 1990). The most common explanation for the warming of the earth's surface is the greenhouse effect, an increase of greenhouse gases in the atmosphere due to an increased use of fossil fuels. These gases (carbon dioxide, methane, nitrous oxide and water vapour) allow radiation from the sun to pass through to earth but act as a blanket when heat, radiated from the earth's surface, travels out into the atmosphere. This is a natural phenomenon without which the earth would cool too much. However, an increase in greenhouse gases has increased the 'thickness' of the blanket, contributing to an increase in the earth's temperature above normal. Dramatic temperature rises could cause changes in weather patterns worldwide and make the earth less livable. It is possible that the production of increased levels of carbon dioxide would also cause greater vegetation growth. It is possible but less likely that ice caps would melt, seas would rise significantly and diseases would increase in frequency.

What is not clear from the studies is the extent of the change and whether it is significant. For a start, global climate varies considerably from year to year. The temperature of the earth can be affected by volcanic eruptions and natural long-term fluctuations due to changes in atmosphere currents, ocean current flow and the luminosity of the sun. So a substantial part of the warming might be attributable to quite natural cyclical phenomena. By the same token, the greenhouse effect may have been larger and some of these factors may have reduced its effects.

Although there seems to be general agreement that there has been an increase in temperature of the earth over the past century, some commentators suggest that much of the data could be unreliable (Jones & Wigley, 1990; Hoyt,D.V. 2000; National Research Council of the National Academies, 2000). Some parts of the earth have not been well monitored by meteorological stations especially parts of the Southern Hemisphere. Changes have also occurred over time in the design of instruments, observation methods, location of stations, formulae for calculations, and the environment of stations especially in urban areas. Although some melting of glaciers and sea ice have been recorded, a study of tree rings does not support warming for the last twenty years.

Other evidence leaves questions unanswered. Why is it, for instance that, while data suggests an increase in temperature at the surface of the earth, it also indicates that the eight kilometres of atmosphere above the earth shows no appreciable warming? Why are lengthy periods of cooling interspersed amongst the general warming trend? Why is it that the earth warmed more rapidly between 1920 and 1940 than greenhouse models would predict? Why did the earth cool between 1940 and 1970 even as greenhouse gas production was increasing rapidly'? (Jones & Wigley, 1990.) These anomalies could be attributable, of course, to other natural fluctuations but they also diminish the strength of the argument that global warming is significant and that greenhouse gases are a major contributor to any warming effect.

The fuel contributing most to greenhouse gases (the fuel with the most carbon) is brown coal, followed by black coal with natural gas the least offensive fossil fuel. Countries that rely on uranium and hydro-electricity might worry less about polluting the atmosphere. However, all countries have cars, a major source of greenhouse gases. So, a general trend of increasing temperature should be a cause for concern for all governments and they are, quite rightly, attempting to tackle the problem.

☐ The Kyoto Protocol

In December 1997 representatives of one hundred and fifty nations met in Kyoto, Japan to negotiate an agreement about the reduction of emission of greenhouse gases. According to the agreement, developed nations would be required to reduce their emissions over time but developing nations would be exempt from the agreement because imposition of curbs on emission in those countries would slow their development and further exacerbate their level of poverty. However, the greatest increase of emission of greenhouse gases comes from the poorer countries. So the non-inclusion of developing countries drastically decreased the impact the agreement might have on reducing the worldwide production of greenhouse gases.

66 The imposition of a carbon tax would devastate the economy. **99**

Nevertheless, Australia, the US and the governments of the other developed nations set about to see how they might comply with the limits set by the Kyoto agreement. Australia is particularly vulnerable to restraints that might be applied to comply with the Kyoto agreement because its economy depends, in no small part, on the extraction of fossil fuels and their use by industry. Australia is the world's biggest exporter of thermal coal and coking coal, has significant supplies of oil and is a large exporter of natural gas. Its power stations (responsible for about a third of Australia's greenhouse gas emissions) rely, predominantly on the burning of coal. Australia also has industries like steel and aluminium that require substantial amounts of cheap energy to compete on world markets.

There are a number of ways for governments to encourage business and industry to reduce emissions of greenhouse gases. A commonly floated scheme involves a government levying a carbon tax. It has been calculated that, in order to reduce emissions sufficiently, the tax would cause a significant rise in the cost of fuels. In Australia, the price of coal might increase by over 200%, oil by three-quarters and gas by two thirds. The price of electricity might increase by over 100%. The subsequent cost increases for industry have been estimated to be 44% for aluminium, 12% for steel and 5% for iron ore production. With those cost increases, neither aluminium nor steel producers would be able to compete against rivals in non-complying countries or even countries that imposed lower carbon taxes. They would face the choice of closing down or moving offshore to set up business in a non-complying developing country. Such price rises would also make the mining of much of Australia's coal uneconomic, causing the closure of mines and decimating an important export industry.

An alternative scheme that might prove to be more acceptable to Australian industry involves the trading of 'carbon credits'. This is based on the fact that trees absorb carbon dioxide from the atmosphere. So, as the proposal goes, if more trees are planted, they will absorb more carbon dioxide and reduce the concentration of greenhouse gases so reducing the dangers of global warming. Companies with hectares of trees would gain carbon credits. Companies producing or burning fossil fuels would purchase credits in proportion to the amount of fuel they burned. The impact of such a strategy on global warming is debateable, however, especially when the act of planting a tree releases carbon gases into the atmosphere. It has also been calculated that, if Australia keeps planting trees at the current rate, it will offset only 3% of its greenhouse gas emissions by the year 2008. Nevertheless, in August 1999 the Sydney Futures Exchange announced that it would begin trading in carbon credits by mid-2000. Those that hold large holdings of trees, such as state government forests, stand to benefit from such a scheme. A private Australian company plans to plant large amounts of saltbush in semi-arid salt-prone areas with the potential to be traded for carbon credits. The saltbush scheme has additional merit in that it should help rehabilitate land that has been degraded by clearing and subsequent contamination by salt from a rising water table. Major international oil companies support the carbon credit scheme. Buying carbon credits will add to their overheads but, by economising in other ways, they should still be able to operate at a profit. Such a scheme should force fuel suppliers and users to reduce consumption (so decreasing their need to purchase credits), use less polluting fuels and seek alternative 'green' energy sources. Some oil companies are already spending a lot of money researching 'green' energy sources, especially solar energy.

The Australian government has other means available to it to force the reduction of greenhouse gas emissions. The transport sector contributes nearly one fifth of global air pollution. Mandating direct injection engines, supporting the development of fuel cells and demanding greater use of ultra-light materials could reduce pollution. Such initiatives would significantly increase the price of cars. Power generation from the burning of fossil fuels also makes a major contribution to pollution. If the certainty of increased air pollution were considered less acceptable than the faint possibility of a nuclear accident, nuclear power could be progressively introduced as an alternative form of power generation in the country. However, public opposition to both car price hikes and nuclear power are likely to prevent either idea becoming reality in the near future.

At the time of writing the US senate voted unanimously against accepting the Kyoto Protocol unless major developing countries also agreed to reduce emissions. Australia has said it won't sign the agreement until the US does. It, along with Japan and Canada, oppose penalties being applied. The European Union, which draws a considerable proportion of its power from nuclear sources, is prepared to sign an agreement in 2002.

☐ Alternative Energy Sources

If Australia converted to power from sources other than carbon it could reduce its greenhouse gas problems. Australia has vast sources of uranium, the fuel for nuclear reactors. But uranium is unlikely to be used in Australia until the antipathy of the public is overcome (see Energy: Is Nuclear Power the Answer?). Three other possibilities are being explored for commercialisation. The first involves solar energy. Solar panels have been around for years but they are expensive and devices hitherto have only worked well when the sun is shining. That problem may now be solved. A team from the Australian National University (ANU) has developed a device that uses a parabolic dish to concentrate enough solar energy on a reaction vessel containing ammonia to break it down into hydrogen and nitrogen gases. These gases are then stored for later use. Any time (day or night) the hydrogen and nitrogen can be recombined to produce ammonia along with a considerable amount of heat. The heat is then used to produce steam to run a steam turbine and the ammonia is returned to the solar reaction vessel to be broken down again and again. No chemicals are lost to the environment and the source of energy is the sun. The ANU team has calculated that 3600 square kilometres of dishes would be needed to supply Australia with its electricity requirements. How much this would cost was not revealed.

The second method, wind power, also has had a long history. You need a frequently windy place to make the system viable. Pacific Hydro thinks that Victoria is windy enough to set up its first wind farm costing $30 million and serving 15 000 homes in and around Port Fairy. An incentive for further such developments comes from the federal government that recently announced that all electricity suppliers must purchase an extra 2% of their power from 'green' sources by 2010.

The last method is probably the most ambitious. It relies on the fact that, four or so kilometres below some parts of the earth's surface, granite rocks exist at a temperature between 200 and 250 degrees Celsius. Two promising areas are thought to be in the Cooper Basin and in Queensland. You drill two holes down into the granite rock about 500 metres apart. Then you pump cold water down one of the holes. It squeezes through the hot granite to the other hole where it is pumped to the surface as steam. The steam is then used to run a conventional steam turbine to make electricity. The Australian National University and Pacific Power have been given a government grant to explore the possibility of setting up a hot rock power station in the Hunter Valley where the hot granite layer may be as big as 100 square kilometres. The Energy Research Development Corporation believes that there is sufficient hot rock in Australia to keep it supplied with electricity for thousands of years. However, don't expect too much energy from this source for some time.

☐ Other Environmental Issues

According to a 1998 Australian Bureau of Statistics survey about the environment, Australians are most concerned about pollution of air, fresh water and oceans. Destruction of forests, garbage disposal, the ozone layer, toxic chemicals, the greenhouse effect, soil erosion and salinity and the loss of wildlife also featured highly. Although all these issues are serious, three have been prominent in news reports over the past year.

Salt

The clearing of native trees by farmers to make way for crops and pastures has caused water tables to rise with the threat that it is only time (between 50 and 200 years) before the land becomes salt-affected and useless for traditional farming. The problem arises because ground cleared of trees allows more water to seep into the soil. The extra water cannot seep away quickly enough causing the ground-water to rise, bringing salt to the surface. There is a possibility that some rivers (including the Lower Murray river that provides water for Adelaide) will become salty within the next fifty years making the water undrinkable and useless for irrigation. So far schemes to slow the spread of salt show little effect. One solution would be to undertake a massive tree planting operation. It is estimated that it would need to cover between 30% and three quarters of the land surface depending on the region. Such a scheme has been started in Western Australia and has the support of farmers who see pine trees as a future cash crop. Another government initiative involves prohibiting further clearing of land.

Poisons

More Australians die from poisoning in the workplace than from suicide or on the road. A University of Sydney study blamed exposure to substances like asbestos, pesticides, solvents, dusts and carbon monoxide for death or major incapacitation. Lung cancer and tumours were common together with kidney, heart and nerve diseases. There is a clear need for greater education of both workers and management with greater penalties for management that do not ensure protection of the workforce.

Wildlife

Population growth, pollution by big business, hunting for food or profit and deforestation for logging or settling, have all contributed to the destruction of habitat and extinction of animal species around the world. Stocks in more than 50% of freshwater species are declining and marine life is under threat from over-fishing. Around Australia the seas are becoming more polluted with urban waste, farm run-off and unlawful cleaning of tanks at sea. Not only is salt-affected land becoming a problem but other land has been contaminated by chemicals designed to control pests and weeds. Over-grazing, soil erosion and damage by feral animals exacerbates the problem. However, there are signs that farmers, clearly aware of these problems, are finding ways to rehabilitate and conserve their vital resources.

References

Hoyt, D.V. (2000). Greenhouse Warming: Fact, Hypothesis, or Myth? http://users.erols.com/dhoyt1/index.html

Jones, P.D & Wigley, T.M.L. (1990) Global Warming Trends, Scientific American, August 1990.

National Research Council of the National Academies (2000). http://www4.nationalacademies.org/news.nsf/isbn/0309068916?OpenDocument

ENERGY: IS NUCLEAR POWER THE ANSWER?

☆ Main Points

The world continues to demand more energy and countries are forced to make difficult decisions about how best to meet that demand. Australia is in an enviable position. It has vast quantities of fossil fuels, uranium, sunlight and other sources of energy. Utilising each of these energy sources has its advantages and disadvantages and deciding on Australia's energy future presents a complex problem for governments.

✓ Executive Summary

Australia has the largest deposits of coal and uranium in the world and is blessed with lots of sunshine. Yet increasing domestic demand for electricity combined with future restrictions imposed by the Kyoto Protocol have meant that government, industry and commerce must make some difficult decisions about the future of supply of energy in Australia. Although coal is plentiful and cheap, burning it in power stations is a major contributor to greenhouse gases. Natural gas is cleaner but it is also piped directly to homes and businesses as a fuel. Australia has already exploited the most suitable sites for the production of hydro-electricity. Solar power, wind power and geothermal energy have great promise but are likely to be expensive to exploit and currently contribute a negligible amount to electricity production in Australia.

This leaves nuclear power plants as an option. Uranium is plentiful in Australia and mines and modern nuclear power plants incorporate many safety features. Danger to the public could be minimised. However, there are a number of seemingly insuperable problems with the adoption of a nuclear power program in Australia. There would seem to be widespread public antipathy to even the mining of uranium, let alone its use in power stations. Secondly, the cost of building nuclear facilities would be very expensive and would require substantial private investment. Lastly, it could take between five and ten years to build a nuclear power station and a large number of coal fired stations would need to be replaced by nuclear facilities if greenhouse gas emissions were to be reduced significantly.

❖ The Big Ideas

☐ Consumption

Although global energy consumption dropped slightly in 1998 (BP-Amoco, 1998), the demand for energy worldwide, especially electricity, is likely to continue to increase as the world population continues to increase and as developing countries become more industrialised. The generation of electricity represents 40% of the world's primary energy consumption and the World Energy Council has predicted that the demand for electricity will triple by 2050 (ElBaradei, 1999). In the industrialised world, energy consumption can be placed in categories such as transportation, home, business, industry and farming. As oil products become more expensive it is likely that public transport will rely more on trains (and trams) that run on electricity. Both the home and business are becoming increasingly hi-tech with more and more devices running on electricity. To remain competitive industries are automating their plants and run them twenty-four hours, seven days a week.

☐ Sources of Energy

Fossil fuels, including coal, oil and natural gas and the burning of biomass produce 63% of the world's electricity. Nineteen per cent comes from hydro-electricity. Seventeen per cent comes from nuclear power with less than one per cent from other energy sources.

Coal

Australia has the largest reserves of coal in the world and these reserves are readily accessible and reasonably easy to mine. So it is little wonder that burning coal provides 82% of our electricity. Although it is an inexpensive source of energy it is now something of a liability because the burning of coal releases carbon gases into the atmosphere. This not only pollutes the atmosphere but contributes to global warming (see Global Warming).

" Into the foreseeable future, 'green energy' is unlikely to produce any more than 15 percent of Australia's energy needs. **"**

Oil

Oil is not used much commercially for the production of electricity because coal is cheaper and more plentiful. Oil has many other uses, for instance, as a lubricant, for which it is indispensable.

Natural Gas

Seven per cent of electricity in Australia comes from the burning of natural gas. It is a cleaner fuel to burn than coal so is more environmentally friendly. It is also piped to homes and industry for use as a fuel.

Hydro

Ten per cent of Australia's electricity is hydro-electric. Major hydro-electric schemes require considerable amounts of flowing water, usually through artificial dams. It is unlikely that Australia will produce much more hydro-electricity since the major sources have already been exploited.

Uranium

" According to the Electricity Supply Association of Australia there is no way renewable resources can deliver any more than 15 per cent of the total electricity generated. **"**

Ian Hore-Lacy, Uranium Information Centre.

Australia has about a quarter of the world's easily accessible uranium ore. Kazakhstan has 19% and Canada 14%. South Africa, Namibia and Brazil also have significant ore bodies. Jabiluka Uranium mine, situated close to Kakadu National Park and Olympic Dam in South Australia are the two major Australian uranium mines.

☐ Alternative Energy Sources

Solar Energy

Solar hot water heaters have become ubiquitous in Australia. In a country with plenty of hot sun like Australia they work well, even in the southern states. As long as they are used consistently for a number of years the initial costs to a house-owner of installing a solar hot water system can be offset by the production of cheap hot water thereafter. Hitherto, the problem has been in up-scaling solar power to be commercially viable for the production of electricity. Photovoltaic cells can be used but are too expensive for wholesale commercial electricity generation. However there are some interesting developments in this area with the use of a reaction involving ammonia gas to store energy (see Global Warming). Even if such a method were successful it would take years to set up enough solar units to contribute significantly to Australia's energy supply.

Wind Power

Of course wind generators need to be set up in places that get strong winds regularly. Denmark, for instance gains 3% of its electricity from the wind. Typically, wind farms consist of fields of propellers on stilts that are spun as the wind blows. A commercial wind farm is currently slated for development near Port Fairy (see Global Warming).

Geothermal Energy

Some parts of the world, such as New Zealand and Iceland, have places where underground water comes into contact with very hot subterranean rock. The water or steam that comes to the surface can be used to run steam turbines. Australia has a number of areas where subterranean hot rocks are reasonably close to the surface. Plans are afoot to bore holes into this rock, pump water down the holes and collect the heated water for a steam turbine (see Global Warming).

Tidal Power

Some parts of the world, for instance the Bay of Fundy, in Eastern Canada, have very large differences between high and low tides. This gives rise to the flow of massive amounts of water which can be harnessed to turn turbines to produce electricity. Australia has no commercial tidal power plants.

These alternative energy sources contribute less than one per cent of the world's supply of electricity. The World Energy Council suggests that, even in the most favourable scenario, the contribution to global supply from these alternative sources is unlikely to exceed 6% in the next twenty years.

Fusion

Unlike the nuclear fission (breaking apart) of uranium atoms nuclear fusion (the joining together of small atoms) does not involve dangerous radioactive raw materials. Instead it requires deuterium, which can be obtained from seawater and tritium, which can be obtained from the light element, lithium. Energy is released when these isotopes of hydrogen are compressed together at very high temperatures and pressures. Fusion reactions are the basis of the sun's energy. However, sustained fusion reactions have yet to be demonstrated on earth. Research continues but there seems little possibility of it being achieved in the near future.

☐ The Case for Uranium

As a signatory to the Kyoto Protocol, Australia will need to reduce its greenhouse gas emissions considerably by the year 2008. In a worst case scenario Australia will face penalties, possibly international sanctions, for non-compliance. But how will it comply? Australia relies on the burning of fossil fuels for nearly all of its electricity supply. If this is reduced without other forms of energy coming on stream the result will be catastrophic for industry, the economy and Australia's standard of living.

Windows of opportunity will open over the next fifteen years as old coal-fired power stations are de-commissioned. It has been estimated that, if they were replaced by gas burning power stations, carbon dioxide emissions could be reduced by 25-30 million tonnes. However, a more efficient use of gas is to pipe it directly to houses and industry rather than burn it in power stations. The replacement of coal burning by natural gas, solar and wind energy will not be enough to reduce carbon dioxide levels to those required by the Kyoto Protocol. However, another form of energy is readily available in Australia: uranium.

The same amount of power as produced by the decommissioned power plants could be generated by six nuclear power stations and the reduction in carbon dioxide would be about double that of using gas (Hore-Lacy, I. 1997).

☐ World use of Uranium for Domestic Energy Production?

There are no nuclear power plants in Australia. In the rest of the world, thirty-three countries run a total of something like 440 nuclear power stations. More than three-quarters of the electricity generated in France and Lithuania is from nuclear energy. France generates enough electricity to export some to

> **"**Around thirty years ago there was a debate about nuclear energy as a source of electricity. It was rejected because the cost of building nuclear power stations was much greater than that of conventional coal fired power plants.**"**

Italy, which operates no nuclear power plants. Belgium obtains more than half of its electricity from nuclear power. Nuclear power stations in Sweden, Switzerland, South Korea and Bulgaria produce 40% of their energy requirements. Both Japan and Spain produce one third. The United Kingdom, Germany and Taiwan produce a quarter. The biggest producers of energy from nuclear sources are the United States (670 TWh), France (370 TWh) and Japan (310 TWh). However, there are few plans for further expansion of the nuclear power industry in Western Europe or the United States. There are two reasons for this. There is continued public antipathy towards nuclear power stations. Moreover, money can be made more easily and less controversially by investment in enterprises other than nuclear energy. There are plans for plants in other parts of Eastern Europe and in Asia. Russia has a number of aging plants that will have to be decommissioned and replaced in the next decade. Japan is reported to be planning to have 20 more reactors on-stream within ten years. Nuclear power accounts for only about 1% of China's supply of electricity although this is expected to increase with five more power stations coming on-line. The Lucas Heights facility in New South Wales houses the only nuclear reactor in Australia. It is used for research and for the production of radioactive materials used in radiation therapy in hospitals.

" In the 1980s laws were passed in Victoria and New South Wales prohibiting the mining of uranium and the building of commercial nuclear power plants. "

❑ Obstacles to the Development of Nuclear Power Stations

There are major obstacles to Australia adopting nuclear power as an option. There is widespread resistance to the use of nuclear power in this country. Any political party that facilitated its introduction would have to be very convincing or risk a groundswell of voter displeasure. Laws in New South Wales and Victoria even prohibit the development of nuclear reactors and the mining of uranium. The costs of importing specialised equipment and building nuclear power plants would also be very high. In OECD countries the costs of generating electricity from nuclear power are nearly the same as from burning gas or coal. In Australia, nuclear power would be 10% more expensive - making it much less attractive. Investment would need to come from private enterprise, which would also have to deal with concerted harassment from environmental demonstrators. Power plants would take between five and ten years to build.

☐ Mining Uranium and the Production of Electricity

If political obstacles could be overcome, there is plenty of uranium in Australia. Once dug out of the ground the ore is crushed then ground in water to a fine powder and sulfuric acid is added to dissolve the uranium oxides. The mixture of 'silt' and solution is left to settle and the liquid containing the uranium is removed. The solution is 'purified' then the uranium precipitated out as uranium oxide. The solid uranium oxide, which is mildly radioactive, is then packed in steel drums for shipment to power stations.

All mining in Australia is tightly regulated by governments, with strict environmental protection measures required of operators and with large fines for infringements of environmental regulations. All miners are bound by an agreement with government to rehabilitate the land when mining is complete. Minimum impact means cost savings to the mining company. There is careful monitoring of the processes for treating material left over after the useful uranium is extracted. The 'silt' left after the extraction of uranium from its ore will still contain some radioactive material. It is mixed with water and pumped to a tailings dam where it is treated with barium chloride to take any radium present out of solution. Radium in the tailings decays to form radioactive radon gas. To reduce emissions of radon gas the 'silt' is covered with water. At the end of the life of the mine the dam can be covered with clay and topsoil and revegetated. Tailings can also be returned to an open pit and covered with rock and topsoil ready for tree planting. Underground disposal of waste was recommended in a government inquiry, the Fox Inquiry. There is less chance of pollution through leaching and greater protection from radiation.

The operation of a modern nuclear power plant is sophisticated. Remote monitoring and automation means that labour costs are low and operation procedures are relatively simple. The latest designs require no human intervention in the case of an emergency but rely, instead, on natural properties like gravity for shut down. The generation of energy follows simple steps. Fuel, in the form of pellets of uranium oxide is put in steel tubes and loaded into the reactor vessel in which graphite moderator rods and coolant have

" Mining 30 tonnes of uranium and refining it to produce electricity could reduce emissions of carbon dioxide by one million tonnes. **"**

already been placed. Uranium atoms spontaneously emit fast neutrons along with large amounts of heat energy. The neutrons collide with other uranium atoms causing them to emit more neutrons and more energy and, if enough uranium is present (a critical mass) this results in a nuclear (fission) chain reaction. The moderator slows down the neutrons to better control the reaction. The heat from the reaction is then used to produce steam to run turbines that generate electricity. After some time the nuclear fuel is spent and needs to be replaced. This spent fuel is highly radioactive and will remain so for many years. It is stored for later disposal. The big problem is where in the world it can be disposed of.

" The permanent storage of nuclear waste would only make sense if a geologically stable site could be found far from living things. Where in the World could that be? "

☐ Should Australia Sell Nuclear Waste Storage Facilities to Other Countries?

Disposal of waste from reactors is a growing concern for countries with nuclear power stations. The waste is still highly radioactive and will be so for a long time. Although the amount of waste annually is not large, stockpiles of stored waste increase with each year because nobody wants the waste 'buried in their backyard'. Some people have suggested that central Australia is a prime candidate for nuclear waste disposal. They say that the geology is stable and places can be found that are far from human settlement. Australia has also developed a substance, Synroc, a synthetic rock that promises to be the best material for the containment of nuclear waste material.

There are already plans to dump the small amounts of low level Australian nuclear waste in a specially designed site in the South Australian desert. In another development, Pangea Resources (a US company) approached the Federal Government in 1999, with a proposal to build a facility in Australia to accommodate high level nuclear waste from nuclear reactors worldwide. Although this could be highly profitable to Australia ($3 billion in royalties to state and federal governments over 40 years) the plan has been rejected by the Federal Government. This is probably because it is still unclear whether there are any unpopulated areas of Australia that are geologically stable enough for the storage of nuclear waste and partly because an acceptance of the proposal is unlikely to be looked on favourably by the voting public.

☐ Other Concerns about Nuclear Energy

Accidents and the International Nuclear Event Scale

> " Japan's worst ever nuclear accident [Tokaimura] ....underscores the fact that the nuclear industry poses a serious threat to public health and the environment. "
>
> Friends of the Earth.

Worldwide there are concerns with the safety of nuclear facilities. Accidents such as that in Chernobyl in the Ukraine and at Tokaimura in Japan do not engender public confidence in the safe operation of nuclear facilities. The International Nuclear Event Scale was designed by experts to accurately describe incidents and accidents associated with nuclear power plants. The scale has seven levels of seriousness. The most serious level (7 on the scale) involves a major accident where a release of radioactive material leads to widespread environmental damage and danger to health. The accident at Chernobyl was class 7. A class 5 emergency involves a limited release of radioactive material that needs substantial clean-up. At the same time there may be substantial damage to the reactor core. In 1957, the release of radioactive material from the Sellafield power station in the UK would have been classed as a class 5. So would the 1979 accident at Three Mile Island in the US where a reactor was badly damaged but little radioactivity escaped to the outside. A class 4 incident would involve a small release of radioactive material to the outside but dangerous exposure of plant workers. The 1999 incident at Tokaimura, Japan was classed as a class 4 incident. A class 1 incident would involve workers not being harmed despite using an unauthorised procedure. Reports suggest that class 1 incidents had occurred at Tokaimura prior to the 1999 incident. Apparently attempting to cut corners, the workers at the Tokaimura plant kept on adding uranium to a tank when the regulations stipulated a maximum of 2.4kg should be added. Enough uranium was added that a 'critical mass' was reached resulting in a chain reaction that released huge amounts of energy and massive amounts of radioactivity.

> " Every day around 3,500 people die in China of illnesses attributed to pollution from coal-fired power plants. "

☐ Crunch Time for Government

The Kyoto Protocol puts the Australian government on notice to decrease greenhouse gas emissions quickly. This means reducing the burning of coal in power stations which would also decrease consumption drastically. This would have to be done through the imposition of extra taxes or the artificial raising of prices, neither of which will be received favourably by the general public, business and industry. Alternatively electricity generation from another source must be found. Natural gas is a possible interim solution. However, because it is also pumped to homes and businesses as a fuel, its cost is likely to rise substantially. Unless some miracle can be found in producing large commercial amounts of electricity cheaply from the sun, wind or geothermal energy the only viable solution left would seem to be nuclear energy.

References

BP-Amoco Annual Statistical Review (1998) as quoted in The Australian Financial Review, 17/9/99.

ElBaradei, M. (1999). Nuclear Power and World Energy Needs: Looking Ahead. Fourth Annual Strategic Conference, Institute of International Relations and Strategies, Paris, May 1999.

Hore-Lacy, I. (1997) Nuclear Energy Prospects in Australia. (http://www.uic.com.au/nip44.htm)

TAXATION

☆ Main Point & Executive Summary

With the likely explosion of electronic commerce over the next few years, governments must find new ways to monitor commerce and collect taxes. If governments are not to experience a revenue shortfall, sophisticated tracking of electronic transactions might be required together with international agreements to monitor commerce and cash flow.

❖ The Big Ideas

❑ Adoption of the Internet by Australians

The Australian Bureau of Statistics has reported that by May 1999 forty percent of Australia's adult population had accessed the Internet. This is an increase of over 50% compared to the previous year and makes Australians some of the biggest Internet users worldwide. In the three years from February 1996 to May 1999 the number of adults using the Internet from a home computer increased almost tenfold. By October 1999 there were well over 100 000 Australian commercial web sites and their number is increasing by about 200 a day. About half of all small businesses and over 80% of large businesses were connected to the Internet. Nearly twenty percent of small businesses and nearly half of all large businesses had a home page. At the moment businesses tended to use the Internet for e-mail, advertising and for information gathering and only just thirteen percent had adopted electronic commerce. Nevertheless, if the US, which is supposed to be a year or two ahead of Australia, is any guide, the number of businesses adopting e-commerce will dramatically increase over the next two years.

❑ Taxing Goods and Services & Monitoring Cash Transactions

❝ The networking of supply chains is a major force driving the US economy. **❞**

In Australia, the government levies goods and services taxes, collected by vendors and paid by consumers. But if the vendor is, say, in the United States, the Australian government cannot require it to collect Australian GST. If, for instance you purchase music from a site in another country and make sure that the transaction is encrypted for security, it will be difficult for a government to detect the transaction and charge you goods and services tax.

Governments, worldwide, could face potentially large shortfalls in revenue from the avoidance of taxation on goods and services purchased over the Internet and especially from vendors in countries outside their jurisdiction. Even if a large number of countries enter into reciprocal agreements to monitor and share information about overseas sales, still other countries may offer secure, encrypted banking with low taxes to help tax-avoiders beat the system.

The widespread adoption of e-commerce brings forth questions about how electronic transactions can be monitored for taxation purposes. There are some who believe that it will be very difficult for governments worldwide to monitor e-commerce and collect suitable taxes, especially since a lot of business will be international. Instead, they believe that governments might be forced to ignore the digital world and concentrate on taxing physical goods such as houses and cars.

In anticipation of a significant increase in e-commerce the Australian Taxation Office has written two detailed reports, the second, published in December 1999, on the implications for taxation. The second report quotes OECD estimates that global electronic commerce, starting at a base of 26 billion US dollars in 1996-7 would increase by more than tenfold by 2001-2 and by a factor of 50 by 2003-5. Clearly, if it were difficult to levy taxes on Australia's share of electronic commerce, the Australian government would miss out on substantial taxation revenue.

The report identified some ways individuals or companies might be able to avoid paying tax. They might, for instance, sell products from a web site offshore to take advantage of another country's low taxation policies. Or they might alter their digital records to minimise the amount of tax they paid. They might, surreptitiously, electronically transfer money from Australia to a bank in a tax haven to avoid income tax. They might simply hide the identity of the owners of a web site or hide a transaction by encryption.

" Supplies of services and intangible property to private consumers (from overseas) present potentially the greatest test to effective administration of consumption taxes.**"**

Electronic Commerce: A Discussion Paper on Taxation Issues, OECD Ministerial Conference, Ottawa, October 1998, quoted by Fiona Buffini, The Australian Financial Review, 9/3/99.

" I've had a go and its bloody hard trying to access a piece of paper out of a tax haven of any description. Now think of that capacity across the net! **"**

Quoted by Fiona Buffini, The Australian Financial Review.

Aware of the possibilities for fraud or avoidance, the government is exploring possible avenues for effective tax collection. To prevent the deletion of records the government could require that businesses use electronic transaction software that allows for message digests, checking the integrity of the record, digital certificates to identify buyer and seller and a date/time stamp for each transaction.

If international transactions are to be monitored Australia will need to enter into agreements with its major trading partners. It remains to be seen how easy it will be to gain international agreement in this regard. In the meantime the government has called for a report on how the GST could be collected on goods and services ordered and delivered over the Internet.

Lastly, let us return to the example of the purchase of music over the Internet from a site in the US. The tax office report indicates that little revenue is lost if government foregoes a tax on imports of small value such as CDs and books. For this reason, it would seem that, at least in the interim, goods of low value, imported into Australia from abroad, would not incur tax or import duties.

Part Three:

Living

LIVING THE HIGH TECH LIFE

☆ Main Point

Technology is making a fundamental impact on the way we live, the way we work and the way we play. Technology provides greater complexity and greater choice. Homes become 'wired' and 'smart' while our choice of entertainment expands far beyond placid TV viewing. For some, the working day can expand to 24 hours forcing changes in the way we lead our lives. Twentieth century thinking about shelter, food, privacy and having babies will be challenged and revised.

✓ Executive Summary

The rapid developments in technology will mean that many devices in the home will be capable of remote control. Connections within the home and with the outside world will be seamless and continuous. Those rapid developments will create an increasing divide between the rich and the poor. Crime is also likely to increase.

Work can no longer be compartmentalised. Globalisation and access to mobile technology mean that many people change their work habits. Fewer people work a 9 to 5 day. Professionals work longer hours. Shift workers have breakfast at 4pm. Unless workers or their employers are proactive we will find that stress is endemic. Time for recreation is reduced. More women choose a career instead of having children. Work in the bush pays less than in the city.

It is debatable whether we are better off than we were in the past. Many people report feeling pressured, stressed, have no control of their lives and suffer information overload. We will rely more and more on authoritative information sources for our news. To make best use of our free time some will outsource house cleaning, ironing clothes and washing the car. We will buy more prepared foods and anything we prepare ourselves will be healthy and fast.

Modern technology gives governments and businesses the opportunity to gather information on all aspects of our lives, especially our buying habits. These can then be bought by anyone wishing to sell to a specific market. There are those who argue that such practices make advertising cost-effective, hence possibly reducing the cost of products to consumers. Consumers are also targeted more accurately, so reducing the nuisance of junk mail. However, the development of personal data banks could be seen as a further invasion of our privacy.

❖ The Big Ideas

❑ Your Techno-Smart Home

- When fast, broadband, Internet access is possible home owners might use their internet service provider to store all valuable personal records including digital photos, videos, financial records and legal documents rather than storing them at home.

- Home devices are already becoming more multi-functional to include fax, photocopier, PC, telephone and Internet connections (see Morphing Mobiles).

- Connections with the Internet will be continuous via a cable modem and will be subsidised by advertising. Continuous connection to the Internet via cable modem makes a computer more vulnerable to hacking. Although better protection of home computers will become available, hackers have a habit of rising to the challenge.

- Application Service Providers (ASPs), will make software available for lease on the Internet.

- By 2002 homeowners will be able to install wireless home intranets. This will mean that devices such as TV, air-conditioning or security cameras can be controlled remotely.

- Fear of crime amongst the rich will precipitate the development of secure enclaves in cities.

- Although changes in architectural style tend to lag behind technological change it is likely that house design will increase its sensitivity to energy conservation and increase use of resources such as solar power and natural ventilation.

❑ House Prices

A 1999 report of the Australian Housing and Urban Research Institute predicted that the price of homes in Sydney, Brisbane

> **"** The workforce is dividing into two groups. One consists of people who are paid very well, are skilled and work long hours. The other is made up of people who are poorly paid for unskilled tasks in casual or part time employment. **"**

and Perth would increase by 3% yearly to the year 2030. Price increases in other capital cities would be less pronounced. The small increase in house prices and the impact of the GST will mean that having a rental home may be a less attractive investment than in the previous century. By the year 2030 a quarter of dwellings will be rented.

☐ Your Work

The advent of the Internet has changed the way some of us work and how we relate to time. In the United States only about 30% of workers have regular days working 9am to 5pm. Many do shift work or work irregular hours. Some stock markets and international businesses are in operation 24 hours a day because, what is our night is day elsewhere. We may need to stay up half the night to participate in a conference phone call on the other side of the world. Or we may receive a call for help from a relative in another time zone. Some restaurants, recognising the irregularity of many working lives offer all-day breakfasts. Some hotels (those near airports with strange flight scheduling) offer a room for any 24 hour period rather than the standard overnight stay.

- Because workers are working longer they are socialising less.
- A Japanese study has found that there is a relationship between the number of hours worked and the incidence of heart attack.

> **"** People are stressed because their workload has increased, they are working longer hours with fewer resources and still feel that their job is under threat. **"**

- Because many professional workers are given projects rather than required to work set hours they work long hours at the office or complete work at home in the evenings or weekends.
- The mobile phone, the fax and e-mail mean that a worker can be contacted anywhere and at any time, blurring the lines of demarcation between work and the rest of one's life.
- About 33% of the Australian workforce work between 35 and 40 hours a week.(1998)
- 33% of the Australian workforce work more than 50 hours a week (1999)
- 16% of women (of age 25-54) worked more than 9 hours a day (1997)
- 87% of women feel rushed (1997)

- More than a third of workers work outside of normal working hours.(1999)

Another Solution for Overwork: The French Government Decrees Maximum Work Hours

By law, on 1st January 2000 all French companies with more than 20 employees had to restrict the working week of all employees to 35 hours without a reduction in total pay. In return employees had to agree to a flexible work arrangement where they might be required to work longer hours during peak demand periods to be balanced by fewer hours during slack periods. Although workers are happy they work fewer hours unions indicate that flexible working hours can be stressful. Moreover, those workers who want to work longer hours to earn more now cannot. Some also say that employers are not hiring more staff but simply require existing employees to do the same job in less time.

The Bush

A publication of the Bureau of Social Sciences reported the following statistics:

- Just over half the percentage of rural people held a university degree compared with those in cities.
- In the first half of the 90s there had been a rapid increase in the number of rural people studying for university degrees.
- The farm workforce is ageing
- Incomes are generally lower than in cities
- There has been an increase in the number of women working in agriculture.

Women, Work and Procreation

A 1999 Australian Bureau of Statistics report has identified a commitment amongst both low and high-income women to remain childless. This trend was identified in high income women some time ago but has now become a general trend. Reasons for foregoing having children include:

- Preoccupation with getting ahead in a career.
- Reticence to forego the freedom, pleasures and benefits that come with no children.

- No interest in bearing and raising children.
- Medical reasons.
- Asserting that the world is not a fit place for children today.

Such statistics mean that the retired, baby boomer bulge may need support from a society that has fewer than expected tax-payers. There could be, however, a way of reversing the birth-rate decline. Countries with systems that allow women to combine work with raising children have higher birth rates. One can conclude that, if companies developed work practices that helped meet the needs of working women those women are more likely to decide to have children. These practices might include:

- Help with child care issues
- More flexible working hours
- Paid maternity leave
- Permanent part-time work

☐ Are We Happy?

In 1999 a number of studies conflicted in their findings about the happiness of Australians. There would seem to be prima facie evidence that many Australians are unhappy at least some of the time. One in every five of us will seek psychological help this year. We have one of the highest suicide rates for young males in the world. Drug addiction and violent crimes, road rage and vandalism are all increasing. A recent report from the World Health Organisation predicted depression will be a major cause of illness in the next 20 years.

Too much change tends to bother us and the rate of change, both economically and socially, over the past few years has been great. In a recent survey 35% of respondents indicated that they believed that such change was too fast. Nearly half of all those in the age bracket 45-54 worried about job security and about 40% of people worried about family income. Perhaps being competitive is an enduring human trait, especially amongst men. In a predominately materialist society such as ours, competition translates into a bigger income, larger home, more power and a more expensive car. In a sense, materialists who are competitive can never be truly happy because there is always more for which they could strive.

Many people also feel pressured, with little sense of control. Because we are going through a period of rapid change, organisations are working overtime to keep market share, find a niche or, at the very least, find a firm toehold in the technological and economic revolution. This puts time pressure on many of us who work in or around those organisations. As writers of this book, for instance, we know that developments in society are currently occurring at such a fast pace that, if we don't complete this book soon, much of its content will be passé!

> **More and more the general public expect their information in ten second news grabs.**

☐ Information Overload and a 'Random Accessed View of the World'

TV, radio, newspapers, magazines and the Internet, let alone our friends, provide us with information. CNN presents the news 24 hours a day. We cannot hope to read every word in a newspaper. We find it harder and harder to see the wood for the trees. Faced with a surfeit of information how do we cope? We can learn to skip read, hoping to grasp the big ideas as we do. Our interests act as a filter to the plethora of news around us. We chomp off byte sized chunks of someone else's reality and leave the rest. It is the only way we can cope. But this approach inevitably leaves us with 'a random accessed view of the world'. How can we see a bigger picture? We need quiet time to reflect. Time pressure and information-overload conspire to reduce the time available to us to reflect and analyse. The simple and superficial can easily replace the measured and insightful. We need to develop strategies to put those bits of the world we understand into a wider, context-based picture of the world. Alternatively, we can choose to rely on a small number of trusted sources that summarise the big ideas for us.

> **Wasn't it Einstein who said it was more important to be able to locate information rather than memorise it? He should be living today!**

☐ Outsourcing

In 1999 sixty percent of Australians over the age of 18 participated in some form of physical activity with males slightly more active than females. Walking, swimming and aerobics were the most popular activities. For some people every hour of the day is precious. They do not want to spend their free time doing house cleaning, mowing the lawn, weeding the garden, washing the dog, cleaning the car and maintaining the pool. So they pay others to do the work for them. The most likely clients for home services at the moment are Generation X (25 to 36 year olds) who make up 30% of the population. It is likely that Generation Y (15 to 24 year olds) will follow suit. The service industry also extends beyond the home. Other outsourcing functions include laundries, tutoring and waste disposal.

☐ Eating

Busy couples do not want to cook often so they eat out or buy food to take home. If they eat at home conditions apply:

• Preparation time needs to be cut to a minimum

• A microwave oven is essential for cooking and re-heating

• Cooking utensils must be easily cleaned

• The food needs to be healthy, tasty and nutritious

So a stir-fry in a wok is popular because it meets these needs.

One report last year indicated that sales of fast-food outlets may have levelled off. Many people buy fast-food because it is just that - fast. However, many fast foods are high in fat so the health-conscious are looking elsewhere. Not slow to see this demographic, supermarkets now offer 'home meal replacements', in other words prepared 'healthy meals to go'. Some fast-food chains have responded in kind, offering ' skin-less chicken' and the like. Australians out-source one in five meals.

☐ Privacy

To what extent should privacy be a right in the workplace? A 1998 survey of large Australian companies revealed that employee e-mail was monitored by 13% of companies and 6% read e-mail messages. Companies say they do this so that they can not be made liable for e-mail content coming from their premises. Other companies prohibit private e-mail correspondence in the workplace. Some companies also monitor what web sites employees visit to cut out time-wasting and un-authorised use of computers by staff. These practices might be seen as contributing to the maintenance of an effective workplace.

But fears about loss of privacy extend to the home. Most Australian consumers are at least somewhat concerned about providing personal details online. Companies believe that gaining information about customer buying habits will allow them to advertise their wares more productively and increase sales. When you browse their site they may be able to find out something about you unbeknownst to you. If you place an order they get a lot more information. Your name, address, phone number, interests, income and much more could be shared with other interested parties.

So valuable is information about the interests of web users that there has been a proliferation of companies set up solely to gather information about consumers. When you visit a web site it can, without alerting you, send a small file called a cookie to your computer system. Each site you visit can then be tracked. This information can be collated then sold to on-line vendors. You can delete cookies from your computer but it takes time to do so. There are a number of ways you can find yourself on a list:

- Enter a mail-in competition
- Fill in a questionnaire
- Buy shares
- Order by mail order
- Subscribe to a magazine
- Join a club
- Pay council rates
- Participate in a frequent flyer program

However, we can hide our identity from companies that indiscriminately collect personal information on us. We can do this by 'purchasing anonymity' from an intermediary. To do this we would need to always surf going through the intermediary's site that, for a fee, of course, shields customer data from anyone trying to collect it.

More cause for paranoia?

- A company is taking photos of every house in Brisbane. It can then match photos with previous sale prices and sell the information to real estate agents.

CYBER GOLD RUSH!

" What I'm trying to do is awaken people to the fact that if they are not careful with their personal information they are going to lose it. "

Malcolm Crompton, Australia's Federal Privacy Commissioner quoted by Wayne Smith, The Courier Mail, 23/10/99

- A man in the United States, let's call him Joe, had his wallet stolen. The wallet contained some pieces of identification. The thief who stole the wallet was arrested for other crimes and used Joe's ID when he was arrested. The thief went to jail and Joe suddenly had a criminal record. Such records are distributed to employment agency data-bases throughout the country. In the next few years the real Joe applied for one job after another and always missed out. He now has to carry with him a police letter saying he is innocent of any crime because it is virtually impossible to delete details of Joe's record from all the data bases in the country.

- Personal information such as unlisted telephone numbers, tax file numbers, credit ratings and bank account numbers can be bought over the internet. Even more sensitive information like criminal records and medical history can be bought on the black market.

- Laws to cover privacy in the private sector will be introduced in Parliament next year. Organisations that gain personal information about you will need to gain consent from you before they are able to pass the information on to another organisation.

HEALTH OF THE NATION

☆ Main Point

Although many Australians are overweight they are reasonably healthy. Yet the prospect of an aging population combined with the public demand for increasingly costly modern treatment has put pressure on government and the health industry. Better health education and the use of technology are ways health professionals are meeting the challenge.

✓ Executive Summary

Compared with much of the developed world Australians are healthy but many are overweight. The health problems they face will tend to be inherited from their parents or be self-induced. Faced with this prospect, government and the health industry have decided that a combination of public health education and innovative use of high technology might be the best means of providing quality health care at reasonable cost.

High technology features in many developments in health care. Corporations are, for instance, gathering detailed records on the health of workers to enable timely health treatment with resulting increases in productivity. Home care professionals will access detailed records of patients and be able to consult with other professionals via mobile links to better serve patients. Diagnosis and treatment of strokes could be performed by a nurse under the supervision of a specialist in a far distant city. Advances in technology will allow people to live with a metal pump inside them instead of a transplanted heart.

❖ The Big Ideas

☐ State of the Nation's Health

Australians are one of the healthiest groups on earth, fifth behind the Japanese and inhabitants of a few European countries, but healthier than the British, New Zealanders and Americans. A recent report from the Australian Institute of Health and Welfare makes the prediction that the life expectancy for the average Australian male, born in 1996, is nearly 76 and for females, 81.

Unlike those in less developed nations, we do not die from complications that set in after relatively minor primary infections or injuries. Instead, we either inherit particular susceptibilities from our parents or we do not look after our own health. For both men and women heart disease (25% of deaths) and stroke (10% of deaths) are the main causes of death. For men, these are followed by lung cancer, stomach cancer, suicide and work and traffic accidents. One might conclude that a careless indifference or 'need to be macho' runs as a root cause for at least some of these problems. For women, the next major cause of death, after heart disease and stroke, is breast cancer. Other major causes of death in the population are chronic bronchitis, bowel cancer, diabetes mellitus and prostate cancer.

The major causes of disability in the population are depression, dementia, asthma, arthritis, deafness and alcohol abuse. More women visit doctors with depression than do men but this may be because men tend to be less ready to admit to a problem. A review of reasons for visiting a doctor revealed that visits for hypertension or high blood pressure, upper respiratory tract infections and immunisation were the most common, followed by depression, acute bronchitis, osteoarthritis, asthma, back problems, non-insulin dependent diabetes and high cholesterol.

In the latter part of the twentieth century health authorities realised that public health education might make a considerable contribution to the well-being of the population. Smoking, diet and physical activity have become major targets for education. The United States government estimates that half the adult population is overweight and 20% are obese, with men the more likely to have a weight problem. Researchers suggested the following factors contributing to this trend: lack of exercise, eating out more tended to mean eating more sweet and fatty foods, sedentary work practices, pastimes and general lifestyle. There is evidence to suggest that people who are overweight are more susceptible to cancer, heart disease, diabetes and strokes.

Australian researchers have estimated that two thirds of men and nearly half the women are overweight. Another report, last year, revealed that 33% of Australian children are overweight and are very likely to become obese adults. Many of these children came from families where the parents were overweight. But other factors include sedentary TV and computer entertainment, parents insisting all the food on a plate be eaten and parents feeding children food that they liked, not what is healthy.

The sexual health of men was the subject of another report in 1999. Between the ages of 15 and 35 testicular cancer was seen as a problem. Once over 35, men can suffer from low sperm counts meaning fertilisation of the egg will become more difficult. Forty percent of the over-forties are reported to have at least temporary impotency problems and, once they are over forty-five the same percentage have urinary problems. By the time they hit fifty, half the male population have impotency problems and thirty percent present with problems of the prostate gland. When they are over sixty, sixty percent have trouble maintaining an erection. The report made no mention of men in older age brackets but one might believe, with all those problems in earlier life, many older men might have become seriously depressed!

☐ The State of Health of the Health System

For some time now the federal government has made it clear that the public health system has limits to what it can support and that, if you want more than this you should invest in private health cover. Currently one third of hospitals in Australia are private, the rest public.

" The efficiency of hospitals is measured by how many nights patients spend in a hospital bed. **"**

There are two major factors affecting the future of the health industry:

• The trend towards a future where an increasing number of retired older people are dependent upon a decreasing number of tax payers.

• An increase in the costs of new drugs and specialised technology.

Faced with increasing financial constraints, government and the health industry have had to develop innovative measures to maintain quality of service. For instance, the federal government has made money available for a 'proactive' initiative that focuses on illness prevention and health maintenance instead of a traditional 'reactive' approach to health care. In the scheme, GPs will be encouraged to increase the number of their home visits to help infirm patients avoid complications or improve recovery. They might also identify health risks associated with the home environment. The idea has been put forward that the first point of call for most patients could be a qualified practitioner in a call centre who had the ability to deal with the problem over the phone or refer the patient to someone who could. In another report it was suggested that the 'cost-saving', early release of women from maternity wards had led to problems mothers had with breast -feeding and post-natal depression.

🗌 Patients Using the Net

The Internet is reported to currently include a quarter of a million medical Web sites and patients are increasingly surfing the Internet for information about specific medical complaints before visiting their doctor. Doctors indicate that, although a percentage of the sites are unreliable, the Internet can be useful. It is important for lay-people to develop the skills to discriminate between reliable sites and the work of quacks. At the surgery the doctor can also help the patient assess reliable sources. The aim is to identify authoritative sources where assertions are backed up by reliable, documented evidence. Surfers should beware of sites that market a particular product or are the opinion of an individual who is unable to support an argument with evidence. Patients are also using the Internet in another way. Individuals in the United States are avoiding visits to their doctor by ordering prescription drugs like Viagra from Internet pharmacies. Customers merely had to provide a short medical history and sign a liability waiver. Medical authorities are concerned that such practice puts individuals at risk through inappropriate usage.

🗌 Doctors Using Technology

Doctors' handwriting has always been the butt of jokes about its unintelligibility. The chance always exists that a misread prescription by a pharmacist could lead to an adverse drug reaction in a patient. So a number of GPs in Australia (estimates range between 10 and 50%) have moved to issuing prescriptions using a computer. This is yet another initiative to make the health industry more efficient.

Over the next few years we are likely to see a more efficient system for support of home health care professionals. This will include the exploitation of state-of-the-art mobile wireless communication technology by health care workers to access patient records and data mining systems and increase collaboration and coordination with other health care professionals via secure private networks. Such technological supports promise to deliver better care to the patient through a more efficient service while still offering considerable cost savings to the health industry.

Diagnoses can now be made at a distance. The longer a victim of a stroke remains untreated the more damage is done to the brain and the more severe can be the paralysis of the patient. Doctors in the United States have profiled a system where a GP or a skilled nurse, at the bedside of a patient, can consult with a specialist, who may be in another city, for the timely diagnosis and treatment of a stroke victim. At the moment the link is via telephone but plans are afoot to provide the service on the Internet.

◻ Corporate Health

An increasing number of companies are introducing corporate health initiatives to improve worker health so decreasing the number of days workers are absent through illness and also increasing productivity. The company would also benefit from a decrease in the cost of health-related insurance claims. Companies argue that a healthier workforce will also be a happier workforce. But there are those who warn that a company collecting the medical details of each worker could constitute an infringement of privacy. Nevertheless, studies of similar programs in the United States suggest that there are considerable benefits to business and society although the return on investment depends on the corporate health program chosen.

◻ At the Leading Edge

Research on artificial heart 'blood pumps' is taking place around the world, including Australia. Some of these hearts are designed as a temporary measure while a replacement heart can be found. Others are designed to be permanent. In fact, by 2005 many heart disease patients may be living without a heart. Instead, they will have been fitted with a titanium pump, powered by a small battery rechargeable every two or three days. Last year, the first of these American lightweight pumps, powered by a small battery, situated under the skin, was successfully implanted. The battery powering the pump had to be recharged every hour but improvements in battery technology should make longer periods between recharging possible soon.

Transplants of many different body parts have now become commonplace, so the news that ovaries can now be transplanted in women has not hit the headlines in many papers. However, the ramifications are quite considerable. For instance, fertility can be restored in sterile patients. Ovarian tissue could be removed from someone being treated for cancer, to be replaced once the patient is well. A woman could choose to have a baby long after the normal age for child bearing. Such scenarios bring with them a number of ethical and legal issues. For instance, the ovaries from aborted foetuses transplant best. But there is widespread opposition to the use of a part of an unborn child to produce another child (see Human Genetics).

BABY BOOMERS REVISE THE STEREOTYPE OF THE OLDER PERSON

☆ Main Point

The reaching of retirement age by baby boomers represents a significant economic milestone in Australia. Either through necessity or choice, a considerable number will continue to work. In terms of buying power, as a 'large bulge in the population', they will exert an influence on the marketplace.

✓ Executive Summary

The baby boomer generation (born between 1945 and 1963) will continue to exist as a significant social and economic force as they move through retirement age. Largely eschewing the retirement conventions of their parents (who received the gold watch and joined the bowls club) they expect a future where they can live the lifestyle to which they have become accustomed. This may or may not mean continuing to work either full time or part time. Current hiring practice is still often biased against the over 45 and it will have to change for society to make use of this group of mature, experienced, skillful, stable and knowledgeable workers. Shortages in certain areas may precipitate such a change in attitude towards the older person.

Trendsetters in the past, the baby boomer generation will still expect its needs to be met. We may expect certain leisure activities like gambling and overseas holidays to further increase in popularity. Although healthier and with a greater life expectancy than previous generations, baby boomers, as they grow older, will need greater health maintenance care such as new glasses and more physiotherapy. Those who have not saved sufficiently for retirement will find their later years less carefree as they have to depend on a modest government pension.

❖ The Big Ideas

❏ The Impact of the Baby Boomers

Between the years 1945 and 1963 over 4 million babies were born in Australia, more than a similar period before or since. They became known as 'the baby boomer generation' and, today, make up nearly a quarter of the Australian population. In the year 2000 their ages range between 37 and 55 and the leading edge of the group are reaching retirement age.

Because they represent a relatively large portion of the population, what they do with the rest of their lives has a significant impact on the rest of Australian society. It would be easy to assume that they will spend the rest of their lives the way their parents did before them. But there are signs that many of the baby boomers have good buying power, have had different life experiences, have a more optimistic view of the future and a different attitude towards retirement. They want to continue to enjoy the same lifestyle and they do not see themselves as old or 'over the hill' at 55 or 65.

❏ Statistics

❝ In line with our policy of seeking employment for those over 40, we are pleased to advise vacancies now exist for professionals experienced in: Finance, Banking, Insurance/Sales & Marketing. Please apply: Grey Army Pty Ltd. **❞**

Advertisement,
Courier Mail, 11/9/99

- In 1999 12% of the population of Australia was over 65 years.
- Over 21% of long-term unemployed people are over 50 years of age.
- By 2015 half of Australia's workforce are likely to be mature aged.
- By 2031 nearly a quarter of Australians will be over 65.
- The average age at which individuals have paid off their mortgage is now over 60 years of age. By 65 ninety five percent of mortgagees had paid off their mortgage.

❏ Baby Boomers and Work

Two reports in 1999 indicated that age discrimination was rampant in Australia. It was common for employers to have the perception that older people were unable to keep up, were inflexible and less productive than younger members of staff. In a Queensland study it was revealed that over 80% of employers reported preferring to hire people between the ages of 31 and 40 while less than 10% preferred applicants in the age group 41-50 for executive roles. The banking and finance sector was a particularly poor employer of people in that age bracket. Yet older people have much to offer. They often have greater experience, knowledge, skills and wisdom, reliability, stability and greater maturity than younger staff. Only in education did these attributes seem to be appreciated when recruiting staff.

Retirement of the baby boomer generation will also have an impact on business and industry. In some sectors of business and industry there may even be shortages. This may well mean that the management practice of letting older members of staff leave (current average age of retirement is 58) and only hiring those under forty will need to be reviewed. There is evidence that a significant number of baby boomers, either through choice or necessity, want to continue working either full time or part time to the age of 65 and beyond. Ambitious young people who see the older person as an obstacle to promotion might resent this. That obstacle might be overcome by casting baby boomers in the role of mentors or hiring them as consultants or contractors.

> **"** Companies have to realise that a 50 year old today may still have lots to offer. Henry Ford was fifty when he revolutionised the car industry with the production line. **"**

☐ Baby Boomers as Consumers

Whether they retire or not, baby boomers are likely to have more money to spend than their forebears. In the latter part of the twentieth century the under 30s were the target for most marketing campaigns. Yet now, because baby boomers represent a significant proportion of the population and also have money to spend on discretionary items, marketers will ignore them at their peril. In their late twenties and thirties the baby boomers were used to being the nations trendsetters. Now that they are somewhat older they know what they want out of life and they feel that they have a lot more life left in them. So they will need to be amused. Gambling, overseas holidays, leisure, smaller cars, looser clothing and books and magazines have been suggested as some areas where baby boomers may dictate fashion and spend their money.

☐ Health Care for Baby Boomers

With significant improvements in health management during their lifetime, the baby boomers are reasonably healthy. As they grow older, health problems will inevitably increase. Therefore, with time, we can expect doctors, pharmacies, therapeutics services, opticians and the health insurance industry to be in increased demand for their services. Governments have made it clear to baby boomers that they need to save for their retirement. If they have not done that their retirement could be a time for skimping and hoping for a lotto win. The remaining workforce, even if it is more efficient than ever, is unlikely to provide the tax base to support the levels of pensions that generations in the past have enjoyed.

A REVOLUTION IN EDUCATION

☆ Main Point

Education discovered the Internet some time ago but it has not been until recently that education and big business have found each other. The fusion of education, business and the Internet promises to transform the way people choose to learn and the way they are taught.

✓ Executive Summary

Big business and the Internet threaten to change the way we teach and learn. We soon will see multinational corporations competing with universities for students. Businesses believe there is gold in education while universities discover the need to become entrepreneurial and commercial. Business programs and those in multimedia, telecommunications and information technology will be targeted first. Operations will be lean, with money poured into the design and content of materials rather than on bricks and mortar. Key selling points for educational services will be the quality of materials, price, convenience and readiness of the provider to cater to the needs of the individual.

Because of the ready availability of information, memorisation is much less important for students than the skills of assessing reliability of sources, interpreting, analysing and making valid conclusions. The role of teachers has also changed. They will become not so much providers of information as guides for student learning or co-learners as they work, together, with students. With limited funds, schools will continue to struggle to keep up with the rapid changes in technology. To cope with this, it is likely that education departments will enter into agreements with manufacturers and application service providers to lease rather than buy hardware and software for schools.

❖ The Big Ideas

❑ Impact of the Internet on Education

Only a few years ago it was just the military and universities that used the Internet. Now, many others access it as well.

Universities routinely use the Internet to communicate with and provide information for their students. But, as in other fields, they realise that their audience can now be worldwide and many universities have started to offer their courses, over the Internet, to overseas students. Seeing the potential for substantial income growth from an expansion of student numbers through distance education there has been a scramble by traditional universities to expand their Internet offerings. At the same time, big business has realised that big money can be made from education.

❑ Business Meeting Education Means Business

Big changes are afoot, especially in the provision of educational programs for the corporate sector. Australia has, for instance, recently seen the adoption of a model used for some time in the US; the corporate university. There are some 1600 of them in the US. Now, such entities as McDonald's University and Motorola University in the US, have been followed by the Coles Institute in Australia. Long a provider of educational services to Australian businesses like Ford and ANZ bank, Deakin University (DU) has entered into an agreement with Coles Supermarkets to act as their broker for a wide range of educational and training programs. Deakin University also plans to offer the same service to corporations in the US. This augments DUs domestic offering of a wide range of corporate programs that make up the backbone of the university's profile. Deakin University is not alone in forming liaisons with business and industry. Woolongong University, for instance, has formed a joint research venture with industry to develop the means of mass-producing superconductors. Similarly, the University of Queensland has received substantial funding to bring the Molecular Bio-sciences Institute to the forefront in the field of biotechnology.

The commercialisation of education is no more evident than with the listing of the University of Phoenix on the New York Stock Exchange. Courses offered by these sorts of universities are those with high demand and tailor-made for the busy professional, needing to 'keep up', who is prepared to pay a premium for convenience. Typically set up close to the Central Business District, a 'campus' will provide a small number of lecture rooms and computer labs and a lecture schedule that fits around the other commitments of a professional - early morning, evening and weekend seminars and plenty of high quality take-home materials. Such campuses can minimise overheads by hiring guest lecturers and part-time tutors rather than having full time staff and choosing not to provide the ancillary services offered by regular campuses - such as a cafeteria, bookstore, bank, child care and sporting facilities.

With the same market in mind, Melbourne University (MU) has started Melbourne University Private, a full-fee paying adjunct to MU with schools of multimedia, telecommunications, information technology and energy and the environment. It will operate in buildings separate from the main university but will rely on MU for quality control of curriculum materials and the supply of some lecturers. It plans to cater for the continuous upgrading and requirements for leading edge learning of the corporate sector. At the same time MU has formed an alliance with 17 other research-rich universities around the world (including the Universities of Queensland and New South Wales) to share resources and work on joint projects. The formation of the group has attracted the attention of some multinational corporations interested in joint ventures, including, it would seem, the development of multimedia for education.

There are plenty of other courses, especially in computing software and web design, which can be accessed and assessed over the Internet without a student even setting foot on campus. One student guide describes distance learning programs offered by nearly 900 US universities and colleges. These often have no time limits for completion, allowing students to pace themselves according to their other commitments. Students will often choose courses where they learn skills that they can immediately apply to their current jobs, meaning skills can be re-enforced by regular practice. Executrain Virtual University has recently set up some trial web sites in Australia that will offer simultaneous instructor-led training in such software as Microsoft Office, for large numbers of a company's employees. The instructor, at a remote site, appears on a closed circuit TV via a satellite link and communication can take place with students and lecturer via Internet phones. The advantage for companies is that employees can remain at work while being trained.

Reports suggest that many large companies will soon recognise the profits that can be made from a foray into education. Armed with plenty of Internet 'grunt' they could bring together the world's best instructional designers, web designers and the best professors in major fields to produce 'best practice' Internet learning materials. Support these with tutors in call centres around the clock and you have a worldwide 24 hour-7 day-a-week education system brought to you, perhaps, by a consortium of major multinational corporations. With the same course being offered worldwide, high quality courses could be offered to students at bargain prices, the course completed without time limits, at home.

Customisation might, however, be difficult! But not for the world's largest specialist IT training company, SmartForce (previously CBT systems). The company offers courses on major software systems with students able to talk with lecturers and other students on-line. Student progress is monitored by lecturers so that further information can be fed back to each individual student for remediation purposes.

❏ The Commercialisation of the University

Although Australian universities with sound reputations can expect growth in the overseas market, they are facing some major challenges on the home front. While many European nations continue to provide substantial financial support for universities, the policy of the Australian government has been to reduce its support, making universities become more self-sufficient. By 1997 universities were expected to raise something like a third of their funds from sources other than university grants. These funds had to come by the winning of research grants, the commercialisation of intellectual products or from consultancies and other services to business and industry. So it is just as well that, about the same time, businesses have started to approach universities for their knowledge and their ability to supply it at competitive prices. Some universities have jumped at the chance. Others, not used to dealing with commercial customers, have some learning to do in meeting the needs of corporate clients. Most universities have had to tighten belts and improve efficiencies including providing classes throughout the year, in three terms, rather than the traditional two semesters. This also means that, by studying throughout the year, students can graduate more quickly than before. One piece of good news, however, is that some experts are predicting near universal higher education by 2020.

Although the Federal Government has progressively decreased the funding per university student in real terms, it has become involved in other education initiatives. For instance, with Australia facing a severe shortage of personnel to fill jobs in telecommunications and information technology, it is likely to support the development of an Institute of Information Technology and Telecommunications. With these industries' landscapes changing so fast, educators need help in predicting emerging skill requirements. The Institute will broker provision of up-skilling of workers in these industries and, at the same time it hopes to attract more workers to these fields.

The outcome of all these changes is that those with access to the Internet are likely to be able to make choices from a dazzling array of learning opportunities. Quality of content, price, convenience and readiness to customise will be key discriminating features. Campus-based education will not die. It may remain the learning experience of choice for certain human-interaction skill-development courses such as teaching and theatre arts and for those students who like a routine and schedule or who best learn by face-to-face communication with peers and lecturers. But for many students (currently 25% of Australian postgraduates for instance), distance education courses, serviced by print material, video and on-line notes and supported by bulletin boards, chat rooms, discussion forums, email and telephone contact with tutors, will be the learning mode of choice.

❒ How the Internet has Changed Teaching and Learning

Both students and teachers have needed to adjust to the Internet as a different source of information and means of communication. Educators report that the vast volume of information now available on the Internet presents students with both opportunities and challenges. After learning some fundamental search strategies it is not difficult for students to find information on just about any topic. The difficulty they face, however, is in developing the skills necessary to assess the validity and reliability of sources and then interpret and analyse data to produce a paper that is fresh and insightful with thoughtful judgements, positions or decisions. Memorising content becomes much less important than being able to identify reliable information and using it appropriately.

As with many other professions, the work of teachers has changed dramatically over the last decade or so. Devolution of responsibility by government to schools for curriculum decision-making and financial management has placed greater demands on teachers. They also seem to have become de-facto advisers about students' social problems. At the same time teachers find that 'chalk and talk', once the mainstay of many lessons, is insufficient in keeping the attention of students. Brought up on a diet of TV, videos and the Internet, students expect there to be an entertainment flavour to their lessons. So the Internet has influenced the way teachers help their students learn. For instance, streaming video and on-line data allow students to conduct virtual field trips.

Teachers also find that they are no longer the fount of all knowledge. So they have had to learn new skills as they change their role to that of 'learning coaches', helping students search for, interpret and apply knowledge obtained from a wide variety of sources. One of the greatest benefits this has brought to schools is the partial demolition of the traditional hierarchy of the classroom. With the Internet, it is just as likely that the student knows more about processes and some sources than teachers, so that students become teachers and teachers become learners or co-learners.

The continuous evolution of hardware and software makes it expensive for schools to provide students with the latest in technology. Some schools have chosen to forego ownership and, instead, lease equipment. Elite schools require students to buy or lease laptops. Either way this need to keep abreast of technology adds more to the costs of education. In the near future we can expect departments of education to enter into agreements with Application Service Providers for the provision of software to all public schools. Access to the Internet reinforces, once again, the inequities in education. Students with ready access to the Internet at home are at an advantage in their ability to gain the requisite skills associated with using the Internet for gathering information and for communication.

To help to overcome these inequities some schools are allowing students to borrow laptops for home use.

Although the Internet is a rich source of information, and computers can be fun for students, research has found that too much computer use has its disadvantages. Reports suggest that students who choose to spend too much time with their computers instead of playing physical outdoor games with friends may not develop a three dimensional perspective. This includes the ability to estimate depth and distance and the speed of objects. Experts suggest that children should be encouraged to use their five senses by playing ball games, climbing trees and touching and picking up the objects in their environment so that they learn concepts such as weight and volume.

☐ Education and Work

Education has been slow to respond to changes in the world of work. Too many high school curricula have, in the past, been devised with the goal of preparing students for entry to university. Yet this is simply inappropriate for many students. This has led to schools broadening the scope of offerings to students allowing them to prepare for a much wider range of careers. In the United Kingdom, for instance, the Technical Vocational Education Initiative offers high technology courses like biotechnology, robotics and satellite communications. 'People' people can find courses in the media, child-care and tourism. The artistic can study textiles and industrial design.

The Australian Student Traineeship Foundation (ASTF) has also been a successful scheme. Workplace training typically involves a company taking the responsibility for training a student for a day a week over two years. With workplace learning incorporated into their study program, students also begin to see the relevance of some of their school learning to the world of work. The student learns what it is like in a particular field while employers have access to a wider range of suitably trained potential employees. In addition, some students, who may not have achieved well in school, are given positive feedback by employers for what they are able to contribute in the work arena. So it seems a pity that the ASTF has reached the end of its trial and may not be funded again. Last year about 80 000 Australian students left school without completing years 11 and 12. Nearly half of those leaving school early will be jobless. Without further training they will be very lucky to get anything but the most menial job and many are likely to face long term unemployment.

In a plan to retain more students at school to the end of year 12, the Queensland government is considering giving students a much greater choice of subjects and levels at which to learn. The plan involves allowing students the opportunity to take some subjects in high school and others at TAFE or university. The argument is that students are more likely to want to continue learning if they can pursue subjects that they are good at. Specially targeted will be students in lower socio-economic areas where the dropout rates are as high as 75%.

Thirty years ago smart kids pursued careers in mathematics and the physical sciences. Now they choose careers in computers and business. Mathematics, physics and chemistry are considered too hard and simply 'not sexy' and nowadays scientists are generally undervalued and under paid compared with other fields. This trend has also resulted in a severe shortage of mathematics, physics and chemistry teachers in high schools. The irony is that, while students in schools avoid mathematics and the physical sciences they see a future in the emerging fields of biotechnology and nanotechnology. So, after studying biology and, perhaps multi-strand science in high school, they choose to study biotechnology and nanotechnology at university despite fairly advanced, chemistry and physics being the basis for an understanding of these fields of study.

HIGH-TECH ENTERTAINMENT

☆ Main Point

Digital technology is set to revolutionise the way we are entertained. For instance, the economic health of recording companies may well be threatened by the provision of high quality digital recordings on the Internet. Interactive TV may renew our interest in TV. On-line gambling will become very popular. There will also be intense competition between TV companies as they fight for the right to broadcast popular sporting events.

✓ Executive Summary

The great thing about the Internet is that it is so readily accessible. You no longer need to leave home or the office to receive information or buy things. Music is now easily accessed over the Internet via a number of competing methods. Currently, a lot of material is being illegally copied but technology will soon be widely available to encrypt artists' work forcing music lovers to purchase rather than copy illegally. Downloading directly from a site on the Internet threatens to cut into the profits of record companies let alone record stores. The new regime will, however, be of benefit to performers who will gain a much greater share of the profit from sales. Customers might expect lower prices as well as better access to free demonstration recordings over the net.

By comparison there are much greater hurdles to the widespread adoption of digital TV. This is partly because the price of a digital TV is likely to be about $8000 with little chance that the price will come down in the foreseeable future. Although picture and sound quality will be superior to the current analogue regime it is the feature of the system that allows viewers to interact with their TVs (for instance choosing from which camera angle to view the penalty kick) that makes digital TV attractive. Other issues include debate about which of two competing digital formats to adopt and competition between many companies for space on the digital broadcast spectrum.

The Internet is ideal for on-line gambling. You can watch a golf tournament and bet on such minutiae of detail as whether a particular person would hole a particular putt. There will be casinos open on-line twenty-four hours all around the world. However, such casinos will be a boon to villains for laundering their ill-gotten gains.

If you like reading books the electronic book is just around the corner. The proliferation of electronic magazines and newspapers will reduce the need for paper for newspapers. News-agents may need to diversify.

Popular sporting events will continue to attract vast TV audiences and hence decent revenue for TV companies from advertisers. There is likely to be much greater competition between TV stations for the right to broadcast attractive sporting events. Because of the high costs associated with acquiring rights to these events, we are likely to see different events offered by a wide variety of companies rather than being concentrated amongst relatively few.

❖ The Big Ideas

❑ Music: MP3 May Kill CDs

For some time now it has been possible to download music from the web. This function of the web has become so popular that it is reported that music is now searched for more frequently than pornography. One of the most accessible means of doing this is by downloading compressed digital audio files stored in a file format called MP3. An MP3 player can easily be downloaded from the MP3 web site and downloaded music files with excellent sound quality can be played on a computer. The ease with which all this can be done has considerable ramifications.

- Illegal copying of material is commonplace.

- Recording companies are suing sites for breach of copyright.

- Recording companies are developing an encryption system for storing and down-loading music to protect copyright.

- Unknown artists can find exposure to new markets.

- Portable devices are being developed for playing digitally recorded music.

- Widespread defection of artists to the web from recording companies is possible.

- MP3-download may replace CD-purchase as the most popular means of obtaining recorded music.

- Clever advertising strategies will be needed to enable an artist to gain attention given the millions of music offerings that will be available on the web. An attention-getting band name or song name will be vitally important.

Artists will put their work on a site by:

- Recording their work, converting it to an MP3 file using software free from the web, then sending the MP3 file to the site for posting.

- Sending a CD to a site for encoding.

◻ HDTV & Data-casting

Over the past few years the Australian government has been deliberating about one of the most difficult technical decisions it has had to make. HDTV (High Definition Digital Television) which allows viewers to interact with a program, is considered by some to be 'the next big thing' in entertainment. Pictures and sound quality are better than the current analogue televisions but HDTV sets will cost as much as $8000 with little likelihood that prices will decrease significantly, even in the long term. Because the costs of introduction of HDTV transmission technology would be high, the government agreed that, if HDTV were to go ahead, free-to-air television companies would be given exclusive rights to broadcast HDTV programs in the digital spectrum from the beginning of 2001 until around 2006-7.

Many commentators believe that, because of the high cost of HDTV sets, uptake of the system would be slow with estimated market penetration of HDTV sets at only 5% by 2008. Certainly, the US has experienced a slow uptake of HDTV. SDTV (Standard Definition TV) is a cheaper, but technologically inferior alternative to HDTV. The picture and sound would not be as good as HDTV but sets would only cost between $2000 and $3000. Britain has adopted SDTV instead of HDTV, as its digital format.

If the decision to adopt HDTV was not difficult enough the government's decision was made harder by a group of companies wanting to take up some of the digital spectrum for datacasting. Datacasting technology is designed to provide interactive services such as e-mail, online banking, delivery of government health and education services, tele-conferencing and gambling using a standard television.

In December 1999 the Commonwealth Government decided that free-to-air stations would have to broadcast all programs in analogue, SDTV and HDTV formats until the end of 2008, when analogue would be discontinued. Analogue set owners will be able to watch regular programs on their analogue TV set. However, HDTV and SDTV offer much more. Digital TV allows for enhancements such as choice of camera angle to view a sporting event or a pop up window of player statistics. If viewers wish to take advantage of some of these digital enhancements on an analogue set they will need to purchase a set-top converter box costing somewhere between $300 and $1500.

How readily consumers embrace HDTV or SDTV depends on what free-to-air stations can offer in the way of programming and digital enhancements. There is another factor that may slow the rate of adoption of the new systems. To fully appreciate the improved picture quality, consumers will need to purchase a set with diagonal screen measurement of no less than 90 cm, rather more than the common measurement, today, of 51cm. Such sets are likely to cost considerably more than the minimum $8000.

❏ On-line Gambling

Australia is well placed to be a worldwide leader in on-line gambling because, unlike many other jurisdictions, the government regulates gambling quite tightly. Australia's physical casinos will benefit from their good reputation when they venture into on-line gambling. Since credibility is the key to success for on-line casinos. Gamblers need to feel sure that, if they win a lot of money, they will be paid.

It is expected that gamblers will offer baccarat, roulette and blackjack at the same odds as the physical casinos. And on-line casinos can be set up at a fraction of the cost of a bricks-and-mortar casino. They can also cater to gamblers all around the world including publicity-shy gamblers who may prefer the privacy of gambling at home. On-line casinos may prove to be a haven for criminals wanting to launder money because the use of encryption by on-line casinos may make it virtually impossible for police to follow the money trail. On-line and interactive gambling will be difficult to regulate because the parties involved could be anywhere in the world. It has been difficult enough in Australia to develop a national policy. When it comes to international agreements the complexities increase exponentially. Interactive digital TV sports betting may surpass other ways of gambling. Here you would be able to watch a sporting event such as snooker and bet on whether each ball will be potted.

☐ Virtual Books

Perhaps it was because most of us (over ten years old) learnt to read with books rather than from a computer screen. Suffice it to say that, many of us, faced with the task of reading a long document on-screen, hit the print button to get a copy we can handle. But the time is likely to come when many of us will feel comfortable enough to read a book from cover to cover using advanced technology rather than paper. A number of companies are in a race to develop technology for that purpose. Some believe that the ideal product will be made of plastic and have an electronic display but otherwise will look like paper and be inexpensive. In one form of electronic paper the application of an electric current causes millions of tiny balls, each half black and half white, to flip one way or the other to create an image. In another technology an electric current causes white paint particles to flow to the surface of a page, making that area to appear white or are repelled beneath the surface for the area to appear black. In both technologies the image can be deleted and new images applied but the quality of image is said to still be not as good as on paper. Other companies are trying to improve the visibility of on-screen text.

There are those who believe that, by 2014 half of all books will be electronic. And books are by no means the only application. Some weekly magazines can already be accessed electronically over the internet and newspapers are interested in adopting electronic paper technology. If that happens the newsprint industry would be cut out of production and newsagents no longer needed for distribution of papers.

☐ Viewing Sport

" The only live drama on TV these days is sport! That's one of the reasons it is so popular. **"**

If you haven't noticed it, sport has become big business. Some soccer players in England earn more money in a week than most of us earn in a year. A few golfers earn more in a day than we earn in a year. Athletes in many fields can become rich through salaries and deals with sponsors. Television companies see sport, news and movies as the major attractions for viewers and hence, advertisers. The last soccer World Cup attracted a TV audience of one billion viewers. It is rumoured that a 30 second advertising slot during a Gridiron Superbowl game requires an outlay of more than a million dollars. Ideally, broadcasters attempt to tie up a team, the venue where the team plays home games and broadcast rights. However, this is increasingly difficult as more companies compete for a slice of the action. So, in the next few years expect to see:

- more 'virtual advertising' on TV (where a digital 'virtual' image is superimposed onto the camera image of a sporting venue during a sporting event)

- a greater spread of conduits for the transmission of sporting events (such as the Internet and pay TV) meaning that some prime events are no longer offered live on free-to-air TV.

Part Four:

Science

GENETIC MODIFICATION

☆ Main Point

Genetic Modification (GM) involves the introduction of a new gene into a plant or animal to give it improved characteristics. Although this could possibly be of great benefit to farmers and the third world in particular, there are concerns that the ramifications associated with use of the technology are not known well enough and GM products could be a hazard to humans and the environment.

✓ Executive Summary

The artificial insertion of genes from one species into another (recombinant gene technology) can produce enhanced characteristics in the new product. Such characteristics as resistance to diseases, insects and drought promise greater yields and a reduction in the amount of spraying of fields with herbicides and insecticides. As a result farmers can harvest more crop and the product can be of better quality. Other exciting possibilities include the development of very strong materials by production of material using a spider web gene.

However, there is considerable public resistance to the introduction of GM foods. The public feels that they were not consulted nor have they been given sufficient information about GM technology and products. This has led to a backlash against GM products, especially in Europe, where supermarket chains are pulling GM products from shelves. Guaranteeing that all products are absolutely 'GM-free' is a lot harder because it would require the shop-owner to trace products back through food manufacturers, ultimately to farmers. This has led the European Union to allow food with only trace amounts of GM material to be labelled 'non-GM'. Australia is considering a policy of zero tolerance, a plan that might prove to be unenforceable and, because of the costs involved in labelling products, could cause food prices to increase significantly.

❖ The Big Ideas

☐ Genetic Modification

Plants and animals contain billions of cells. Each cell contains a nucleus inside which are thread-like structures called chromosomes. On the chromosomes are sequences of DNA (deoxyribonucleic acid) called genes. Genes work together to run the way a plant or animal behaves in its environment. If new genes are added to a cell the plant or animal may behave differently.

In traditional breeding certain characteristics of plants or animals (for instance the smell of a rose or the size of a dog) can be enhanced. However, this can only be done through time-consuming and laborious selective breeding and only within certain limits. Two breeds of dog can be bred to produce a hybrid but cross-breeding between species is usually impossible. Those crosses that can occur (such as the cross between a lion and a tiger) are infertile.

In genetic modification, a gene can be taken from one species (a bacteria, virus, animal or plant) and introduced into another (a bacteria, virus, animal or plant) to give the modified species new characteristics. For instance, the gene that allows a fish to live in icy water might be transferred to the chromosome of a tomato so that it would not be damaged by a frost. The process can be thought of as 'cutting' a gene from the DNA sequence of one species and 'pasting' it into the DNA sequence of another. The required gene can be 'cut' from a DNA string using enzymes that only react with certain molecules. These genes are then typically inserted into pieces of DNA found in bacteria. Because the bacteria multiply rapidly they can then be used as a factory to produce millions of identical copies of the selected gene. These then can be 'pasted' into the target organism (the one that is to be modified), let's say a plant. A common way to do this is to incorporate the selected gene into a bacterium or virus that is then used to 'infect' the target plant and in so doing, introduces the gene into the plant's DNA. Another method that is simple, reasonably successful and useful with animals, involves using modified sperm to carry the required genes into an egg.

> " (Biotechnology) will transform all sectors of our economy that rely on biology - medicine, pharmaceuticals, agriculture, natural products, waste treatment, bio-remediation and the environment. "
>
> John Mattick, University of Queensland, Courier Mail, 11/9/99.

In most cases, the required gene is only accepted by some of the targeted cells. To determine which cells have been modified a chemical test called polymerase chain reaction (PCR) has been developed. It is hoped that this will replace another, more controversial, method that used antibiotic-resistant 'marker genes'. These were introduced into a target cell at the same time as the required gene. When plants, for instance were subsequently grown in soil 'laced' with antibiotic, all the plants would die except those for which targeting had been successful. Some scientists are concerned that if humans subsequently ate these plants they might also develop resistance to antibiotics.

☐ The Advantages of Genetic Modification

Genetic Modification can be used to replicate natural selective breeding within a species but it can produce the required improvements much more quickly. More controversially, genetic engineering can also be used to add a gene from one species to a completely different species. A gene might, for instance, be introduced to the cells of a plant to improve the flavour, appearance or resistance to disease of the plant. Plants can be genetically modified to be resistant to pesticides or herbicides or become drought-resistant all of which would lead to greater yields of crops, resulting in greater market value.

Genetic modification also enables new products to be made by means other than traditional chemical reactions. For instance, new products can be harvested by collecting the milk from genetically modified goats. Proponents of such methods argue that using goats that graze in fields is more environmentally friendly than production in a petrochemical plant.

☐ Some Unique Products

Spider Web to Bullet Proof Vest

The filaments in spider webs are very strong. If such a material could be collected in commercial quantities it might be useful in making strong fabric. So Canadian scientists have introduced a spider-web gene into goats' mammary cells. The goats produce milk from which milk products are extracted leaving a substance that can be made into filaments then woven into a fabric. The fabric should be strong enough to be used in bullet-proof vests.

> **"** Genetic modification (GM) has the potential to offer very significant improvements in the quantity, quality and acceptability of the world's food supply. **"**
>
> The Institute of Food Science & Technology, http://www.ifst.org/hottop10.htm accessed 31/1/00.

Genetically Modified Cotton

In the United States cotton has been genetically modified to become resistant to insects. This has increased the yields of crops and resulted in three million fewer litres of insecticide being sprayed.

Genetically Modified Foods

Crops like soy, corn, canola and potatoes are used to make a wide range of food products. Soy, for instance, is found in sauces, soft drinks, French fries and candies and canola is used in baby food. In the US, some of these crops have been genetically modifed for some years now. The genetic modification was designed to improve the crop in some way. It is rumoured, for instance, that US scientists have developed a strain of corn that contains all the nutrients needed by human beings, a product that should be useful in times of famine or disaster in the third world.

Monsanto's 'Terminator' Gene

The development of GM crops is very expensive. Once the GM seeds are sold to farmers what would stop the farmers saving seed from the first year's crop and planting them rather than paying high prices for another batch of seed from the seed company the next year? Monsanto believed they could prevent this from happening by including a 'terminator gene' in the seeds. The 'terminator gene' would cause the embryo in replanted seeds to die, forcing the farmer to buy new seeds each year. News of this innovation so angered the general public that Monsanto announced that they would abandon research to develop sterile seeds. As an alternative means of protecting their product the seed company is reported to have used legal action against farmers who saved seeds. Monsanto also reserved the right to find other technological means of protecting its GM products.

☐ Concerns about the Safety of Genetic Modification

There are concerns amongst some scientists that, because the insertion of genes is somewhat random, the introduction of the new gene might alter other functions of a cell in ways that

❝ Once released, the new living organisms made by genetic engineering are able to interact with other forms of life, reproduce, transfer their characteristics and mutate in response to environmental influences. In most cases they can never be recalled or contained. Any mistakes or undesirable consequences could be passed on to all future generations of life. **❞**

Greenpeace, http://www.greenpeace.org/~geneng/ accessed 31/1/00.

are unexpected and unwanted. So, for instance, the colour, size or fertility of the species might be adversely affected. There are those who believe that the methods used in genetic modification might produce food that caused humans to become resistant to antibiotics, have more allergies or be poisoned. The most frequently cited case is that of the 37 deaths and 1000 illnesses in the US in the late 80s from dietary supplements containing L-tryptophan. Although a genetically modified organism had been used in the process, subsequent investigations revealed that the deaths and illnesses were caused by impurities introduced into the product by poor processing techniques and not because a genetic modification had been used.

There are also concerns about the possible contamination of traditional crops by the cross-pollination from genetically modified species planted nearby. Over 10 000 field trials have now been carried out with no apparent effect to the environment. However, there are those who suggest that effects may only appear after several generations. They also point out that large scale planting may not show the same results as the small-scale trials. Finally, there is concern that unexpected outcomes, such as a weed becoming herbicide-resistant or certain insects becoming extinct, might occur.

☐ Public Resistance to Genetically Modified Foods

Genetically modified crops are so ubiquitous that many food manufacturers say it is difficult and time-consuming to keep track of sources. So they are sometimes unsure whether a food contains genetically modified constituents or not. This has led consumer groups to lobby the government to legislate the introduction of labelling of food products to indicate the presence of genetically modified ingredients. A test, polymerase chain reaction (PCR), can identify food that has been modified so that it can be labelled accordingly. Unlike the European Union and Japanese governments, which allow trace amounts of GM materials in foods, the Australian government is considering a 'zero tolerance rule'. Grocers complain that, if a 'zero tolerance' law is passed, many more foods will need to be labelled as GM products. If mandatory labelling is introduced, the food industry believes it will cost between $1 billion and $3 billion with the costs being passed on to the consumer. This may increase the cost of foods by as much as six per cent.

Strong public resistance to the introduction of genetically modified foods has forced some food manufacturers to revert to GM-free crop sources. In Europe, in particular, food chains have decided to clear GM stock from their shelves. GM labelled products just didn't sell. At the same time European plans to plant GM crops for research have been halted. This all follows a still controversial research report describing deterioration of the immune systems of rats fed on GM material.

At the same time, the high crop yields that can be gained have meant that growers in many parts of the world (including Argentina, Australia, Brazil, Canada and the US) are planting GM crops. For instance, half of all soya beans and nearly a third of all corn planted in the US are GM modified. Since GM foods are likely to be cheaper, larger, tastier and hardier, commentators believe that it is only a matter of time before GM products become accepted. In the meantime, scientists, farmers, food manufacturers and government will need to better inform the public about the nature of and risks associated with GM foods.

☐ Substantial Equivalence: A Criterion for Safety

As a means of allaying the fears of the public, food manufacturers have used the concept of 'substantial equivalence'. According to the principle of 'substantial equivalence', a genetically engineered food is deemed to be safe for consumption if its chemical characteristics are essentially the same as the corresponding traditional food. In the US this means that, if a GM food looks and tastes the same as its traditional relative, it is deemed to be 'substantially equivalent'. In Europe 'substantial equivalence' refers to foods that were produced from one or more genetically modified crops but which were subsequently processed or refined. The argument is that DNA and protein from the original crop would no longer be present after such treatments. In Europe, other genetically modified foods would need to be labelled.

❑ What Genetically Modified Crops are Grown in Australia?

The organisation in Australia that controls the genetic modification of materials is called the Genetic Manipulation Advisory Committee (GMAC). The GMAC has approved the growing of genetically modified cotton in Australia. GM canola is being tested and applications have been submitted to the GMAC for the trialing of herbicide-resistant soy, corn, potato and sugar beet.

In July 2001 the Australian government's Office of the Gene Technology Regulator will open. It will perform environmental impact assessments on all genetically modified organisms proposed for release to the environment.

References

<http//www.environment.gov.au/epbc>

HUMAN GENETICS

☆ Main Point

Biotechnology promises to offer hope for many in the world who suffer from inherited diseases or who need the replacement of a body part to return to good health. Genetic engineering will enable doctors to replace defective or damaged genes with healthy ones without the use of drugs.

✓ Executive Summary

Genetic Engineering promises to bring to medicine completely new ways of treating disease. Hitherto, pharmaceuticals have been used to treat ailments. Finding drugs that are effective for specific medical problems tends to be an expensive, lengthy and laborious process. Although gene therapy is in its infancy it promises a much more direct way of solving many health problems.

A considerable number of the diseases of the world are inherited. This simply means that defective genes were passed on from parent to child. This includes such debilitating diseases as muscular dystrophy and cystic fibrosis. Gene therapy replaces defective genes. Although in its infancy and not without its setbacks, gene therapy promises to treat hitherto untreatable diseases without the use of drugs and their side effects. Genetic research also promises to bring hope to individuals with damaged or defective organs. The technology now exists for scientists to grow body parts from cells provided by the patient.

The human genome project has set out to identify, not only all of the genes that make up the human body, but also the arrangement of the DNA molecules that make up the genes. Possibly due for completion as soon as late 2000, the project should be of great value to all scientists, doctors and corporations involved, in some way or other, in helping people get and stay well. A darker side of genetic engineering involves the possibility that, in the future, parents will be able to choose the characteristics they want in their children. This could precipitate 'intelligence races' between neighbours or nations.

❖ The Big Ideas

☐ Gene Therapy

Some diseases in humans are caused by genetic defects. These include hemophilia, muscular dystrophy, sickle cell anemia and cystic fibrosis. The theory behind gene therapy is that people can be either cured or their lives made better if defective genes can be replaced by healthy genes. There are two sorts of genes. There are those in germ cells (egg and sperm) that, if introduced into a patient, can be passed on by the patient to offspring. And there are genes found in somatic (body) cells that, if introduced into a patient are not inheritable. Since the passing on of these induced genetic characteristics, from one generation to the next, might have unexpected outcomes, most of the work in gene therapy has so far involved genes in somatic cells.

Genes are sequences of DNA (deoxyribonucleic acid) found on the chromosomes in cells. In developing a therapeutic treatment, the appropriate gene needs to be found from the 80 000 - 150 000 or so genes in the human body. The gene then needs to be selected from all the other genes in the chromosome. The required gene can then be 'cut' from a DNA string using enzymes that only react with certain molecules. These genes are then typically inserted into pieces of DNA found in bacteria. Because the bacteria multiply rapidly they can then be used as a factory to produce millions of identical copies of the selected gene. The genes are then ready to be 'pasted' into the appropriate cells of the patient.

☐ Vectors: How Genes are 'Pasted' into a Patient

The method of introduction of the gene into the body must meet three criteria. It must take the gene to the right part of the body. It must transfer the gene in such a way that it can be effective when it gets to the target site. And, of course, the method must not harm the patient. A common way to 'paste' a selected gene into a patient is to use a virus as a vehicle (scientists call them vectors). This is because viruses (which contain genetic material) have perfected the act of invading the human body and they often target specific parts of the body. They, therefore represent a clever vehicle that scientists can use to 'paste' a selected gene into a specific site. The problem, of course, is that scientists don't want to give the patient the illness associated with the virus. So the virus is first modified to make it benign. Then the therapeutic gene is incorporated into the modified virus and the patient 'infected' by injection or by some other means. With any luck, the introduced genes can take over from defective genes and the patient gets better. So far the results have not been perfect. Some times the virus had not been sufficiently weakened and the patient has become sick. Sometimes the patient developed an allergic reaction. Sometimes genes didn't transfer properly and sometimes their therapeutic effects wore off over time. There has been at least one death (in 1999) of a person undergoing gene therapy. In that case, researchers are at a loss to explain the cause of the death, especially since seventeen other patients received the same treatment, using a modified cold virus as the vector, and showed no ill effects. With a continued lack of uniformity of results the initial optimism and excitement amongst gene therapy researchers has been replaced by an understandable caution.

☐ Stem Cell Research

At the very early stages in the development of a human being the fertilized egg contains embryonic stem cells. These cells are undifferentiated, meaning that, at this early stage they are all alike and each could develop into any one of the 210 different cell types in the human body. Perhaps, because of a fear that scientists might use the technique for cloning, the Australian government has banned the use of human embryos for the production of stem cells. But stem cells can also be used to regenerate diseased or damaged body parts, a process that could rehabilitate many people suffering from debilitating or incurable diseases. Scientists suggest that stem-cell treatment will be useful in treating diseases of the brain, the nervous system and bone marrow. Parkinson's disease, for instance, could be treated. Tissue regeneration should be possible in the treatment of those who have lost tissue through major cancer surgery or from burns and for multiple sclerosis sufferers. Damaged or diseased heart tissue might be replaced. Nerve tissue might be grown for patients with Alzheimer's disease. So Australian scientists are lobbying the government for a lifting of the ban on the production of stem cells from embryos. In February 2000 the US National Institute of Health announced that the government would fund research on stem cells obtained from embryos.

In the meantime scientists have found ways to continue with their research. Although there is a ban, in Australia, on 'harvesting' stem cells from human embryos, the importation of stem cells from overseas is legal. The governments of Australia, the US, the United Kingdom and Denmark have also approved the extraction of stem cells from blastocysts (3 day old fertilized eggs). In the first two weeks of its life a fertilized egg contains cells that are all the same. It is not until about the fourteenth day that about half of them become the placenta while the rest become part of the developing embryo. So the cells are technically not being 'harvested' from an embryo since the embryo is yet to be formed. Once the stem cells are obtained from the blastocysts they grow and divide indefinitely in the laboratory producing a continuous supply for research.

☐ Making Body Parts

The demand for the replacement and repair of body parts is enormous. Only one human liver is available for transplant for every ten patients in need of one. Those who have been given the liver of an animal as an alternative therapy have only survived for a week. Now scientists are on the verge of having the capability of meeting the demand. Even whole body parts like fingers or ears can now be grown. Scientists have already grown an ear. The process involves obtaining skin cells from the patient. DNA is extracted from the nuclei of the skin cells and injected into human eggs from which the chromosomes have been removed. The eggs are grown for a week then the stem cells are removed. At this point the stem cells could develop into any body part, so they are treated in such a way that they will become blood vessels and cartilage. The cells are then placed onto a special polymer scaffold in the shape of an ear and left to grow. The ear is then grafted onto the head of the patient. The polymer scaffold and the sutures dissolve in time and, because the body part has the same genetic make-up as that of the patient, there is little chance of rejection.

☐ The Human Genome Project

The genome for an animal is the complete set of design and behaviour instructions for that animal. Animals (and plants for that matter) contain billions of cells. Each cell contains a nucleus inside which are thread-like structures called chromosomes. On the chromosomes are long chains of DNA. DNA is made up of four similar organic bases, adenine, thymine, cytosine, and guanine. But the bases exist in different sequences throughout the DNA. The different sequences provide different instructions for the nature and function of genes. Genes work together to run the way an animal behaves in its environment. So, if we can find out what genes there are in an animal and what sequence of DNA molecules make up the gene, we can better understand how animals, including human beings, function.

It is not quite clear how many genes the human body contains. Estimates vary between 80 000 and 150 000. Whatever the number, in about the year 1990 scientists in the US began the ambitious task of identifying all of the genes in the human body and, even more ambitiously, mapping the sequence of the three billion or so DNA bases that make up the genes. Original estimates suggested that the task would take thirteen years. However, competition and collaboration between a number of research centres around the world, together with advances in technology have meant that the most recent estimate for a completion date is some time in the year 2000. Already, the complete DNA sequence for one of the human chromosomes has been mapped.

However, even when the entire human genome is mapped many mysteries are likely to remain. Researchers from the Institute for Genome Research in the US have just reported the DNA sequencing of the smallest known bacterium, which contains only about 350 genes. Of these, scientists know the function of only 250 leaving the function of the remainder a complete mystery. If the human genome consists of as many as 150 000 genes, it is likely that many mysteries about human life will remain well into the 21st century.

❑ Genetic Enhancement

Genetic enhancement is much more controversial than gene therapy. Suppose you were ready to have children. Many parents would say that all they want for their child is that it will be healthy. However, there are parents who want more. They want brilliant children that are gifted musicians and who excel at sport. They want their children to be tall and beautiful. Very soon it may be possible for them to have all this (at a steep price, of course) through genetic enhancement. There are genes associated with all of these characteristics. If a parent wants their child to have these characteristics all that is needed is for a scientist to replace unwanted 'dumb', 'un-coordinated', 'short' and 'eye colour' genes with the genes that confer the preferred characteristics. So wealthy parents compete for the most genetically perfect child. Nations decide that they can compete better if all of their offspring are smart and good at sport. Once Australians have discovered the right 'cricket genes' they could build a team of champions that could win internationals forever.

Of course, it is not quite as simple as that. Quite a few genes combine to affect intelligence, for instance. Finding the right combination of genes for the child might be difficult because genes interact with each other in complex ways. Choosing the wrong set of genes might result in other, unwanted characteristics for the child. It is, however, sobering to read that a fashion photographer in the US has recently offered, for auction, the eggs of eight of the beautiful models he works with. Apparently one offer of $42 000 had already been received. Some people will do anything to have beautiful babies!

HUMAN CLONING: THE DEBATE

☆ Main Point

Responsible governments around the world have banned bringing a cloned human being to term. The potential risks to the offspring, both physical and psychological, are not known at this stage, but the cloning of animals suggests a number of potential problems for cloned human offspring.

✓ Executive Summary

Adult DNA cloning involves the use of a nucleus from an adult to be used to make 'an identical twin' of that adult. Scientists now have all the techniques to clone a human being. They have already demonstrated the success of their methods by producing cloned sheep, cows and other animals. The success rate is, however, not good and there is the potential to produce offspring with severe genetic defects.

While permitting some strictly prescribed genetic manipulation procedures for therapeutic purposes (see Human Genetics), responsible governments have banned research leading to the birth of a cloned human being. There are a number of reasons for this. Public opinion is against such experimentation. Religious groups believe that scientists are trying to 'play God' and many scientists suggest that the risks of genetic defects in offspring are simply too great. There are also questions about the potential for social and psychological problems in families with an offspring that is both the child of and sibling to one of the parents. Nevertheless, given the unquenchable inquisitiveness of the human race and its natural tendency for competitiveness, it would seem only time before individuals and even nations surreptitiously bring human clones into the world.

❖ The Big Ideas

☐ Adult DNA Cloning Methods

In adult DNA cloning, the nucleus from the cell of an adult will be used in the cloning process. A nucleus is first removed from the cell of an adult male or female (which could be from the cheek or elsewhere) and transplanted into an egg of the female from which the original nucleus has been removed. The egg, with its new nucleus, contains all of the genes necessary to produce a human being. At this stage, however, only the cheek genes (or whatever other cell had been chosen) would be ready to operate, the other genes lying dormant. So the egg would need to be 'activated' with chemicals or an electric pulse to ensure all the other genes were ready to do their job. The 'fertilized' egg could then be implanted into a female to be carried to term in the normal way.

This is not exactly an infallible process at the moment. When they were attempting to clone Dolly the sheep (see below) in this way they tried the procedure on 277 cells and only 29 of the cells started to divide as they should. These were implanted into ewes. Only thirteen ewes showed signs of pregnancy and from these, only Dolly came to term.

Dolly the sheep was born in 1997, the first cloned animal to be born. The nucleus used was from a six year old (that is, a middle aged) ewe's udder. So, when Dolly was born, her cells were already six year's old. She already shows signs of middle age. Because of this she is expected to live no more than another six years.

Because a DNA clone has the same genetic make-up as one of the parents it is likely to share many characteristics with that parent much as identical twins do today. However, because the social and physical environment of the clone will be different from that of the parent they may behave quite differently. The size, strength and intellectual capacity of the clone may also be markedly different from that of the parent.

☐ The Benefits of Adult Human Cloning

In the essay on human genetics we discussed some of the benefits associated with the use of human cells in the treatment of diseases. In this essay we will confine ourselves to a discussion of the benefits, drawbacks and ethical issues associated with bringing a human embryo, developed by cloning, to term.

> " (Cloning) is one of the most exciting and important scientific breakthroughs of the 20th century and should not be prohibited by the government. "
>
> Steve Dasbach, Chairman, The Libertarian Party, quoted in Ethical Aspects of Human Cloning, http://www.ReligiousTolerance.org/cloning.htm accessed 4/2/00.

Scenario 1

Bill and Mary want to have children but he is found to be sterile. However, they can have a cell from some other part of Bill's body implanted into Mary's nucleus-free egg. The offspring would have Bill's genetic make up. This might be more acceptable to the couple than using a stranger's sperm in an in-vitro fertilization procedure.

Scenario 2

Matthew and Martha dote on their tiny perfect child, Matilda. Then, at the age of six, Matilda dies in a terrible accident. The parents would do anything to have another child just like Matilda. The parents would be able to have Matilda's twin if a nucleus from one of the cells from Matilda's body were introduced into a nucleus-free egg from Martha, which Martha could carry to term.

Scenario 3

June and Joan, a couple in a long-term lesbian relationship wish to have a child. Rather than having a man's sperm artificially fertilise one of their eggs they could elect to have the nucleus from one of them inserted into the nucleus-free egg of the other.

☐ Objections to and Dangers of Adult DNA Cloning

- It is likely that the offspring from adult DNA cloning, even if everything else is normal, will have cells the same age as the donor of the nucleus. This will mean that, although, at birth they may look like a normal child, they are likely to age faster than normal.

- The 'turning on' of genes by chemicals or an electrical 'shock' represents a critical stage in the process of DNA cloning. If even one of the genes was not turned on, the child could have serious genetic defects.

- If the process were perfected we might see both individuals and nations competing in a race to produce babies with certain desired traits. Basketball players might all be three metres tall. Musical and scientific 'geniuses' might be bred.

" Someone is going to do this some day. The question is what control does society want to impose on it? "

Ken Goodman, University of Miami, quoted by Martin Merzer, Sunday Mail, 28/3/99.

" One of the prospects should not be, perhaps should never be, the extension of this technique to human beings... Now that it may be possible we would say it should be prohibited, if necessary, by law. "

Carl Felbaum, President, Biotechnology Industry Organisation, Feb 1997 quoted in Ethical Aspects of Human Cloning, http://www.ReligiousTolerance.org/cloning.htm accessed 4/2/00.

- If adult DNA cloning ever became commonplace the diversity of the human race would be diluted, making it, for instance, more susceptible to disease.

- Many religious groups believe that adult DNA cloning is too much like playing God. They also believe that such offspring would have no soul since they believe that the soul is created when the sperm fertilises the egg. No sperm is involved in adult DNA cloning.

- Let us say that the offspring of the 'union' of Bill and Mary is John. John would look similar to Bill. In many ways John would be more like an identical twin brother to Bill rather than a son. This strange relationship might be difficult for mother, father and son to deal with.

NANOTECHNOLOGY: LITTLE THINGS MAKING BIG MONEY

☆ Main Point

Miniaturisation is a key trend in the manufacture of goods. This means that devices that run inside small gadgets must also be small. Nanotechnologists seek ways of making devices smaller and smaller, such as integrated circuits.

✓ Executive Summary

There is a constant demand to make some gadgets smaller. This has meant that the devices inside gadgets that make them work also have to be made small. Nanotechnology is the study of ways of making small things. It has become a lucrative industry with such devices as integrated circuits creating sales in the hundreds of billions of dollars. A Pentium processor®, for instance, contains something like 4 million electronic switches, each of which is no more than 5000 atoms in length. While the traditional way of making integrated circuits, using optical lithography, has been improved over the years, there is a limit to the fineness of the detail it can reproduce. Other methods will be needed if smaller, more powerful devices are to be developed. At the moment there is no industrial process that can do this although work with electron beams and with molecules made of carbon have some promise.

❖ The Big Ideas

☐ Nanotechnology

Silicon integrated circuits, ubiquitous in the manufacture of computers, were the impetus for the development of a new field of scientific research: nanotechnology. In the year 2000 the sale of integrated circuits will reach US$300 billion, incentive enough for many people to show an interest in the field of nanotechnology. The term 'nanotechnology' is derived from the measurement of length, the nanometre. One nanometre (1nm) is 1×10^{-9} m or 0.000000001 metres. In other words, it is an extremely small distance and nanotechnology deals with extremely small things.

☐ Nanotechnology Techniques

Optical Lithography involves shining light through a screen (called a mask) that contains geometric shapes onto a surface covered with a photosensitive polymer. The pattern in the mask is transferred to the surface. Optical lithography has been a key process in the manufacture of integrated circuits. With increasing demand for smaller and smaller integrated circuits for smaller and smaller gadgets, the makers of integrated circuits are approaching a size limit. Current technology can operate at 2.5×10^{-7} m. The problem is that optical lithography cannot cope with distances shorter than the wavelength of visible light. This 'minimum feature size' is about 100nm or 1×10^{-7} m. If people need objects that require distances smaller than that, they will need to look to methods other than optical lithography.

Finding alternative techniques that are fast, inexpensive and reliable is the focus of much current research. Research seems to be divided into two camps. One camp is trying to adapt the general techniques and processes used in optical lithography in such ways that the 'minimum feature size' barrier can be broken. In fact electron beam lithography can achieve sizes of between 8 and 25nm but only under conditions that are not yet conducive to large-scale production.

The other camp is trying to build structures by manipulating single or small groups of atoms or molecules. Perhaps the most newsworthy achievement by this camp so far was the building of the letters 'IBM' with atoms by a group of IBM scientists. They did this using a scanning tunneling microscope. The microscope enables the operator to 'see' individual atoms in a way similar to you putting your index finger into a black box to 'feel' what is in it. The scanning tunneling microscope moves a very fine metal needle just above the object in the microscope. An electric current in the needle keeps the needle just above the surface, so it moves up and down over hills and valleys. The vertical motion of the needle can then be interpreted and a picture of the object obtained. Not only can you 'see' atoms with a scanning tunneling microscope, you can also move the atoms. The IBM scientists used the needle to drag individual atoms from one place to another to form the letters IBM. However, impressive as these demonstrations are, there are currently severe limitations. Only certain atoms, under specific conditions can be manipulated on specific surfaces. The process is also laboriously slow, making likely commercialisation many years away.

Fullerene molecules show promise as particles that can be exploited commercially. They consist of hollow ball-like cages of carbon atoms of various sizes, the most common of which has sixty atoms in the ball and a diameter of just 0.7nm. This is incredibly tiny, but scientists have been able to coat the surface of fullerene molecules with metals and even insert particles inside the cage. Fullerene molecules are chemically inert, nearly spherical and, unlike many particles, do not cling tightly to each other. Their positions relative to each other can also be changed using a scanning tunneling microscope. They can be made very pure, in relatively large quantities and at reasonably low cost. Scientists see them having a range of functions such as being used as micro-capacitors to store electricity inside a nano-machine. Because of their shape, scientists have some-what fancifully speculated that fullerene molecules might even be used, in combination, as minute sleds on which other, larger, molecules could be transported around a micro-environment.

References

Nanotechnology. Timp, G. (ed). New York, Springer-Verlag. 1999.

Nanotechnology: Molecularly designed Materials. Gan-Moog Chow & Kenneth E. Gonsalves (eds). Washington, DC, American Chemical Society. 1996.

Part Five:

Technology

FIGHTING THE DARK SIDE: HIGH-TECH CRIMINALS AND PORNOGRAPHY.

☆ Main Point

Technology and the international nature of the Internet are being exploited for fraud, money-laundering, breaching copyright, industrial espionage and the widespread distribution of pornography.

✓ Executive Summary

Technology in general and the Internet in particular have dramatically altered the way crime is done in the world. The Internet would seem to be tailor-made for crooks. The Internet makes the world border-less. International financial transactions are so commonplace that the laundering of money has never been easier. Moreover, transactions are very rapid, making it easier to hide a money trail. Photographic reproduction techniques make it easy for criminals to hide by creating new identities. Smart criminals realise that they no longer need to hold up a bank to obtain money. High-tech theft and fraud can be even more lucrative and the sale and use of pirated software is endemic.

Facing these sorts of problems means that law enforcement agencies need to dramatically change. The problems of high-tech crime need to be fought with high-tech solutions. High-tech solutions require law enforcement officers who are as familiar with the high-tech world as the criminals they try to catch. Yet someone with such expertise can earn much more money in private enterprise than in law enforcement meaning that many law enforcement agencies are under-staffed. Moreover, since crime has become international, law enforcement needs to keep pace. There needs to be ever increasing cooperation between agencies worldwide if crime is to be kept in check. Below, are some examples of current criminal activity.

❖ The Big Ideas

❑ Fraud

A 1997 report by the European Union found that international Internet fraud involving such sectors as banking, investment and smuggling costs governments and businesses worldwide $77 billion a year. Fraud in Australia amounts to $3.5 billion. Digital technology enables criminals to easily forge documents. Villains scan an official document like a birth certificate or driver's licence, alter it and print false documentation using a laser colour printer. With false documentation criminals can open bank accounts in fictitious names and create false identities. With false identities criminals can more easily launder money and evade income tax.

Since creating a new identity is so easy financial organisations like banks must rely on additional means to establish better security. Holograms and micro-printing can be included in official documents but even these are open to abuse. One of the best ways to counteract these types of fraud involves maintaining secure samples of a body fluid like blood for individuals and checking the blood of a suspected imposter against the stored sample. The costs of such a security blood bank would, however, be large. An alternative would be to maintain comprehensive files of personal information for checking purposes, but, here, there might be questions of invasion of privacy.

❑ Credit Card Fraud

Credit Cards have often been used for fraud. Credit card information can be obtained by:

- Hacking into data bases

- Intercepting non-encrypted credit card details sent over the Internet

- A merchant feeding a card through a 'dummy' card reader that retrieves the customer's card details.

- Purchase of real credit card numbers and customer details from a web site.

Once the information is obtained it can be used to purchase goods and services. Other forms of credit card fraud include merchants not sending goods that a customer paid for or not refunding money for returned goods. Individuals can ensure greater security by making use of encryption facilities in Internet transactions and only dealing with reputable web sites.

☐ Money Laundering by Criminals

Money Laundering is the practice of passing money from illegal sources through a number of institutions so that the original source of the money becomes obscure.

In 1999, it was reported that billions of dollars had been deposited into an account in a US bank as part of a money-laundering scheme operated by Russian organised crime. The scheme, involving transfers of money between banks in different countries, converted the proceeds of illegal activities such as prostitution into what eventually looked like profit from legitimate businesses.

There are two schools of thought about the ability of law enforcement officers to detect and prosecute cyber-crime. There are those who believe that cyber-crimes are becoming increasingly difficult to detect and criminals even harder to catch. Criminals can use the Internet, for instance, to launder the money between Russia and the US while operating in Australia. AUSTRAC (Australian Transaction Reports and Analysis Centre) has the authority to investigate money laundering and illegal banking over the Internet. In order for it to be effective it must have international cooperation with other enforcement agencies. Law enforcement officers can be hampered by having to conduct investigations in foreign jurisdictions with different laws in each country. Even if police are sure that they have cornered 'Igor the launderer' he can transfer incriminating data over the Internet then delete his computer files even while the police are trying to break down his door. Data can now be encrypted making the task of detection even more difficult. Pornographic images, for instance, can be transmitted within other, innocent, pictures. Some police admit they do not have the resources to deal with the problem. The Australian Federal Police Force, responsible for the investigation of international crime and sophisticated computer crime has been forced to reduce the number of investigations it undertakes because of an exodus of experienced officers to better paid jobs. There are other law enforcers, however, who believe that they now have the technology to catch cyber-criminals.

☐ Theft

A study by Rand has revealed that up to US$9 billion annually is lost by manufacturers and their customers through the theft of high-tech products and parts. The majority of product losses were in transit with some losses amounting to more than US$100 000. Rand recommended improvement in the tracking of products, introducing methods to disable goods if stolen and more research into the methods used by thieves. It should be possible to prevent the theft of software by incorporating into the software disabling technologies that can only be turned off with a key provided by the software maker.

☐ DNA Testing: A Breakthrough for Crime Detection

DNA, or deoxyribonucleic acid contains four compounds, cytosine, guanine, adenosine and thymine. These compounds are linked in different combinations in very long strings. At various places in the long string these combinations repeat themselves. Sometimes there are two repeats together. Sometimes there are as many as twenty repeats together. People differ in having different numbers of repeats. These differences can be used for the purpose of identifying the individual. Forensic scientists look for the number of repeats at nine different places on the strings. The chances of any two people having the same set of repeats (called a DNA profile) is something like 100 million to one. This technique has already been used to convict murderers by comparing their DNA with DNA found in samples at the crime site. It has also been used, in some cases, to bring about the release of those wrongly convicted.

By the end of 2000 a national data base will be established made up of the profiles of offenders, suspects and volunteers. Prisoners in jail for more than five years might also be asked to give samples. DNA samples will be obtained from the mouth swabs of suspects. To obtain these, consent is not required in

" At last law enforcement agencies have the upper hand. We now have the technology to monitor cyberspace and can follow criminal activity. "

the Northern Territory but some other states require a magistrate's order. Legislation requires that samples be destroyed for suspects proved innocent. However, there is concern amongst civil libertarians that this may not be done.

☐ Hacking and Security

Hackers are individuals who by one means or another are able to infiltrate the computer system of another individual or organisation. They may attack sites for a variety of reasons. Some say that they just like the challenge of exposing security gaps in sites. Others have sought revenge for being sacked by an employer. Still others, having successfully hacked into a site to extort money from a business by threatening to expose security lapses. Vindictive hackers could vandalise a site by, for instance, changing a company's hyper-links to pornography sites thus potentially damaging the company's image. Or they can simply destroy or temporarily disable your site. Some hackers hide programs in e-mail attachments that, when opened, install software in your computer that allows the hacker to control your computer remotely. One such hacking group claims to have moved telecommunications satellites and hacked into the Pentagon and other government agencies. Other tricks involve forging e-mails to disrupt operations or to cause suspicion and unrest in the workplace. If a site is violated everyone in the company becomes a suspect which, in turn, can lower morale.

☐ Page Jacking

This is where a miscreant copies a web page and uses it for his or her own ends. Here is a scenario. Joe wants to make a killing on the stockmarket. He buys up 2 cent shares in a stock. He then copies the web page of a reputable financial advisor and alters it to suggest that big developments are around the corner for the 2 cent stock. The stock increases in value to $1 and the miscreant sells his shares and makes a killing.

In a celebrated case miscreants copied and altered a large number of legitimate sites. When these sites were accessed people were automatically redirected to porn sites. Once at the porn site the "back" button of their browser was disabled. When they tried to quit, more porn pages were displayed. This process, called 'mousetrapping', was repeated as many as twenty times before the user was able to escape.

☐ Crackers

Producers of software, music, video and other intellectual property find it easy to sell their products over the Internet. But security for these products can often easily be broken enabling software to be down-loaded, copied and sold in another country. Crackers believe that all information set out on the Internet should be free. Crackers, otherwise known as warez, tell others how to obtain illegal software. They give out passwords so that commercial software can be downloaded. It has been estimated that over a third of all software used in Australia is illegal. In some countries with non-existent or weak copyright laws the vast majority of software used has been illegally copied.

☐ Pornography

It has been estimated that about 1.5 percent of Web sites worldwide contain pornographic material. They are very popular and porn sites represent a quarter of the top 1000 sites visited by Australians. An NEC research study found that even the most comprehensive of search engines index only 16 percent of Web sites. Sites can spend time and money increasing their ranking on search engines. One technique used by porn sites to attract visitors involves a careful choice of Meta tags. Meta tags are placed at the top of all web pages, invisible to a reader but detected by search engines. They are designed to provide descriptions of the content of a site. Let's say that one of the most popular sites on the Net is about cooking. It might have Meta tags like 'cakes', 'menus' and 'recipes'. So, as well as including Meta tags such as 'naked' and 'nude', porn sites could also include Meta tags that are used by the most popular non-porn sites. They might include 'cakes' and 'recipes' as Meta tags for their porn site because they know that this will draw in more visitors to their sites. It works both ways of course. You could attract more people to your own home page by including Meta tags such as 'nude' and 'naked' even though your site was perfectly respectable!

◻ Censorship of Pornography in Australia

A law, passed by the Federal government last year brought into force the blocking of porn sites beginning in 2000. The plan requires Internet Service Providers (ISPs) to provide protection of minors from offensive Web material. The proposal requires ISPs to offer filtering services to customers to block access to porn sites. Complaints about offensive content will be referred to the Australian Broadcasting Authority which can order ISPs to block certain content.

Critics of the law can see loopholes. For instance:

• Since private e-mail is exempt from censorship, Web pages could be accessed via e-mail.

• The law exempts 'broadcast delivery' meaning that anyone could access a pornographic Webcast.

• It will not be long before Australian subscribers will be able to gain direct access to the Internet via satellite by purchasing a receiving dish, so circumventing the need for an Australian Internet Service Provider and Australian censorship.

Opponents of the government plan for censorship of the net believe better alternatives include education of responsible individuals such as parents and teachers.

MORPHING MOBILES

☆ Main Point

Through the first six years of the new century the major features of mobile phones, personal computers and electronic organisers will be combined in small wireless units of ever increasing sophistication to provide voice, data and picture communication including e-mail and continuous connection to the Internet.

✓ Executive Summary

Small, mobile communication devices, looking like a cross between a mobile phone and an electronic organiser are destined to become the major vehicle for communication early in this century. Already on the market is the Nokia 7110, a mobile phone using a key to scroll down a screen and capable of receiving 'modified' versions of web pages and of reproducing text and black and white bitmap images. Ericsson and Alcatel also sell mobile phones with a larger than normal screen and fold-down keyboards.

❖ The Big Ideas

☐ Services

❝ Mobile phone high speed Internet access to services and information, any place and any time, will revolutionise all that we do. **❞**

Besides all the features that phones and Internet access currently provide (such as voice mail, e-mail, access to banking, on-line shopping and sharemarket transactions) the new devices will provide paging and access to TV and radio. Tracking technology would enable the user to gain help with street directions and information about, for instance, restaurants in the locality. TeleBackup will provide remote wireless mediated back-up for data stored on mobile communication devices so that, if a device is lost or stolen, the data is still recoverable from a remote server.

☐ Trends

The cost of mobile phone calls has dropped in most parts of the world except Australia. However, as new networks enter the market and as more people use mobile phones, prices will drop significantly, some predicting by as much as 80%. It is predicted that, by 2002, half of all Australians will own a mobile phone. By 2003 two-thirds of all voice phone calls will be over a mobile network and sales of portable Internet-enabled devices will be greater than that of desktop computers. Most mobile devices will be permanently connected to the Internet. By 2003 providers in Europe, a leading trial area for mobile phone technology, will be able to offer customers broadband streaming video and stereo. By 2004 nearly all mobile phones sold will allow the customer to access the Internet and other services. However, with rapid advancements in technology, users who wish to take advantage of the latest advancements will be forced to regularly replace their mobile communication devices with more advanced versions.

Footnote: There is ongoing debate about the habitual use of mobile phones constituting a health hazard.

☐ Technospeak

So you want to learn technospeak. Here is a brief run-down on some of the latest buzzwords to impress and baffle your friends. We've tried to keep it simple, but hey, if you are describing jargon you can't keep the jargon out!

- **GSM (Global System for Mobiles)** controls the Australian digital mobile network. If you have a GSM phone you are in luck! Travelling abroad, you can already get GSM coverage in over 120 countries including all of Europe. You won't be as lucky in the United States where different regions use different systems at the moment. Japan also uses its own system.

- **CDMA (Code Division Multiple Access)** is designed for mobile phone customers who are unable to use the digital network. It has replaced the old analogue network. It is said to offer better coverage and voice quality than GSM.

- If you are planning to go to the North Pole a **satellite** mobile phone might be the answer for you. They can be used to make calls from anywhere on or around the earth. But GSM can already do this, apart from a few very remote places. So check whether a GSM phone will suffice. Satellite handsets are currently very expensive!

- **GPRS (General Packet Radio Services).** If you use a mobile network that uses GPRS your data transmissions will get to their destination ten times faster than GSM networks. GPRS breaks a message into parts, each part travelling on the fastest route to be reassembled at the destination.

- **WAP (Wireless Application Protocol).** WAP is a system that allows web pages to be viewed on screens on mobile phones, pagers and personal organisers. However, you won't get the quality of image on the mobile screen that you get on a PC. This is because WAP converts the content of an Internet web page into text and only bitmap images that can be viewed on a mobile screen. WAP can be run over both the GSM and CDMA networks. However, WAP is not yet a global standard. The first WAP services were launched in Australia by Nokia in 1999. By 2004 it is expected that 95% of mobile devices will be WAP-enabled.

- **'Roaming'.** So you've signed up with a carrier that offers great service but only in your local area. Now you are going interstate on business. Carriers can make their company more attractive by offering the ability to 'roam'. Let us say that a carrier (let's call it ATel) does not offer a nationwide service. It can enter into an agreement with another carrier (let's call it Btel) to 'roam' onto BTel's network in areas ATel does not cover.

- **Portability:** You want to transfer your business from Atel to Btel but you want to keep your phone number? Britain and Hong Kong have had this service some time ago. Australian carriers are not far behind.

- **Bluetooth wireless technology** is designed to allow you to use a lightweight headset to communicate with a mobile phone 10m away. This means that you can wander around your office or go down the corridor without carrying your mobile with you. Calls can also be initiated from the headset by voice recognition. It is predicted that, by 2004, three quarters of all mobile devices will be Bluetooth-enabled.

- **Home Zoning or Local Zoning** allows a customer to make and receive calls on a mobile at fixed line call rates when the mobile device is 'at home'. If the mobile device is a significant distance from home, mobile phone rates apply. The customer may require different numbers for the two services.

- Lastly, three forms of technology have been developed to enable large amounts of data to be transferred rapidly from office to office. Firstly, **3G (third generation wireless technology)** allows you fast access to the Internet via your mobile phone. It combines high-speed mobile telephony and Internet data transmission. 3G will be launched in Japan in 2001 and in Australia in 2002. With 3G high quality streaming video and transfer of large amounts of data become possible. Secondly, **LMDS (Local Multi-point Distribution Service)** is a wireless local telephony network using microwave technology with the ability to transmit business data over a broad bandwidth. AAPT has the only LMDS licence in Australia. Lastly, **CBD Fibre Optic Networks** have been built in capital cities connecting CBD buildings via 'fibre optic rings' enabling rapid transmission of data between nodes in the network.

TELECOMMUNICATIONS: SOOTHSAYERS AND SEDATIVES NEEDED?

☆ Main Point

Telecommunications is the fastest growing business in the Australian economy as it participates in the development of the convergence of phone, data and cable traffic. At the same time, the need to act quickly and think globally has put great pressure on management and has precipitated a massive round of mergers, alliances and takeovers.

✓ Executive Summary

Telecommunications companies are in the business of transmitting voice, data and all other electronic communication. Their core business could be thought of as local telephone calls, long distance calls, mobile telephony, data transmission and the Internet. However, some see their role as also encompassing various forms of entertainment such as TV.

Telstra, Optus and Vodafone own digital mobile phone networks, based on GSM (global system for mobile) technology, in Australia. Telstra has an analogue service but this will be replaced by CDMA (code division multiple access) technology by the end of 2000. There are also a host of resellers of mobile services who buy access from the carriers and on-sell to customers at competitive rates. A number of smaller companies will soon roll out their own local mobile networks, catering to the business markets in Sydney, Melbourne and Brisbane. By 2002 some predict that 50% of customers will own a mobile phone (see also Morphing Mobiles).

A study of Telstra, as the biggest of the telecommunications companies in Australia, offers an insight into the issues confronting large telecoms. Telstra plays on both the domestic and global stages. Domestically it has decided to not only strongly defend its traditional position as a carrier and telephone service provider, but it plans to expand its role in the entertainment field. If it wants to be a player in the global telecommunications field, Telstra needs to form an alliance with influential, and like-minded telecoms overseas. In the meantime it has formed a number of alliances and investments in other companies to improve its technological advantage. In such a competitive market companies are always looking for an edge over rivals. It is likely that the main differentiation between companies, in the future, will be in price, services offered, quality of customer service and reliability of the network.

❖ The Big Ideas

❑ Deals in Telecommunications

Competition is hotting up! MCI-World Com, the world's fourth biggest telecommunications company buys Sprint Corporation, the world's sixteenth biggest telecommunications company with the object of bundling together local and long distance calls, cable, wireless and high speed Internet services; a one-stop-shop offering that should help increase market share. British Telecom, the world's sixth biggest telecom, forms an alliance with Microsoft to develop Internet and multimedia services for laptops and mobile phones. Cable and Wireless (the world's seventeenth biggest telecom)-Optus enters into an agreement with Commerce One to create an Australian portal so companies can buy from and sell to each other worldwide. The National Australia Bank forms an alliance with AT&T (the world's third biggest telecom) and British Telecom to develop the bank's information technology. In Australia, Cable and Wireless-Optus now have a fibre optic cable running between Brisbane, Sydney, Canberra, Melbourne, Adelaide and Perth and have entered into an agreement to lease a link from Brisbane to Cairns to start in 2001.

" Corporations are realising that, to remain competitive, they may need to form alliances or merge. **"**

This is the world in which Telstra (the world's eleventh biggest telecom) must operate. It, like many other large companies, competes with rivals for a position in emerging markets. Telstra cannot develop all of the technology themselves. So they enter into a range of business agreements, often forming alliances with other big companies or taking equity in smaller companies that they believe can help them accelerate the achievement of their goals. At any one time large, multinational companies have in place, perhaps thirty or more arrangements with other companies ranging from loose alliances to takeovers. Last year, a number of Telstra agreements or possible agreements hit the headlines. Telstra had talks with Oracle (the world's second biggest software company) to develop Internet services in Australia through Big Pond TV. Telstra entered into an agreement

" This is all about partnerships and relationships. It is the way this industry is going. **"**

Telstra spokesperson, quoted by Helen Meredith, The Australian Financial Review, 4/11/99

" Because the future is so uncertain, companies are taking positions in a wide range of start-up businesses with the expectation that some, at least, will be synergistic and profitable. **"**

with Nortel (the world's fifth biggest supplier of phone infrastructure equipment) to help Telstra improve its Internet profile. Telstra formed an alliance with Motorola to develop global e-commerce initiatives. Telstra also invested in Sausage Software to help develop 'business-in-a-box' web sites for small businesses. These are only a few of the deals that such companies as Telstra and Optus enter into all the time.

☐ The Rapidly Changing Environment in Telecommunications

All telecommunications carriers face a world where new developments in technology mean frequent change. Here are some examples:

- Telstra already offers high speed Internet access via cable and satellite. However, late in 2000, Telstra plans to offer an alternative high-speed service on the existing copper wire network. Called Asymmetric Digital Subscriber Loop (ADSL), it allows a user to access the Internet at high speed while also using the wire network for telephone calls. Subscribers would need to replace their modems with ADSL ones (manufactured for Telstra by Alcatel) costing somewhere between $150 and $600.

- The volume of data traffic being handled by telephone networks is dramatically increasing. In 1997 data traffic volume between the United States and Britain became greater than voice traffic. By 2001, in Australia, data traffic will equal voice traffic and by 2004 data traffic will be double voice traffic. In response to this burgeoning of data traffic Telstra is changing its network from circuit switched technology to packet-based technology. Packet-based technology allows all forms of communication (voice, data, video, music and so on) to travel together along the same 'pipe' (the conduit for transmission, traditionally twisted copper pairs of wire but increasingly fibre optic cables).

- In order that 'pipes' can cope with increased traffic volume a system (wave division mutiplexing) is being developed that involves sending simultaneous messages through fibre optic cables using a range of different wavelengths of light.

- Telstra also wants to offer a competitive cable Internet service. At the moment it uses an HFC (hybrid fibre coaxial) cable network. The modern standard for cable transmission is DOCSIS (data over cable systems interface specification). So Telstra has called for tenders for some organisation to reconfigure the Telstra cable network.

- Last year Telstra started a service to support the Asian 'voice-on-the-Internet' market. Voice-on-the-Internet (VoIP) is a low cost alternative means of communicating compared with conventional telephony. The system converts voice into data which is then transmitted over the Internet and turned back to voice at the destination. The system, although cheap, is considered by many as producing inferior sound quality. The service will not be offered in Australia, to protect Telstra's existing telephone business.

☐ Selling the Product

- With deregulation of the telecommunications market, competition between companies is fierce with profit margins decreasing. Telstra has drastically decreased the fee to customers for accessing its Internet service via broadband cable and satellite. This is to meet competition from other Internet service providers.

" Telecommunications companies are making sure that they are 'in the face' of consumers wherever they are looking for information or are communicating. "

- Telstra plans to open about 200 Telstra Retail Shops throughout Australia before the end of 2000 to sell Telstra products and services.

- There is evidence that suggests that many large companies change the telephone company they use depending on the price of the service. Telstra, Cable and Wireless-Optus and other telecommunications companies will attempt to win back such customers by 'bundling', offering a range of services together, thus simplifying billing.

- By the year 2010, some people predict that rationalisation will have taken place within the telecommunications industry resulting in only three or four global carrier groups. Telstra has yet to join such an alliance. These alliances, offering 'global brands' will each provide a wide range of services from which customers will select personal packages. Choice of brand will then depend on such factors as price, services offered, quality of customer service and reliability of the network.

- Telstra has broadened the view of itself from being a world class telecommunications company to being a company that deals in all features of transmission. This has led it to consider further moves into the entertainment and sports spheres beyond its part ownership of Foxtel.

- By entering into an agreement with a number of smaller technology companies Telstra is developing a portal for its Internet service that, it hopes, will be so attractive and will meet customer needs that it will drag people away from other portals.

- Both Telstra and Optus plan to participate in a big way in e-business. The business-to-business market is expected to be huge. Optus, for instance, has formed an alliance with a US company, Commerce One, British Telecom in the UK, NTT in Japan and SingTel in Singapore, to form a network of portals for international business.

SMART CARDS, ELECTRONIC CASH & SMART OPERATORS

☆ Main Point

Multi-function Smart Cards promise to offer consumers improved access and convenience when making financial transactions as well as gaining easy access to a wide variety of other services and information. Although some obstacles, like concerns about privacy and security, need to be overcome, pundits predict widespread adoption of smart cards over the next three to five years.

✓ Executive Summary

Smart cards differ from current swipe cards by including a microchip in the card. This allows for the storage of much more information than before and makes provision for secure on-line transactions. All the uses for current cards can be brought together, if necessary, on one smart card. Personal computers will incorporate smart card readers so that business can be conducted on the Internet. Cash will slowly be replaced by electronic cash, stored on a smart card, and replenished on the Internet or at ATMs.

Australia has not adopted smart card technology as fast as Europe, which should see dramatic growth in the next two or three years. Part of the reticence to adopt the technology has revolved around concerns with privacy and security. The encryption technology used in smart cards should allay these fears. However, widespread adoption is unlikely to take place until smart card use becomes commonplace in major transportation networks and for phone services.

❖ The Big Ideas

❏ Multi-Function Smart Cards

We are all familiar with credit cards, video store cards, fly buys cards and the like that use swipe technology. Smart Cards can store much more information than swipe cards and, at the same time, offer the user much better security against fraud. There are stories, for instance, of vendors taking a customer's credit card and swiping it through a device which copies the swipe details so that they can later be put on a forged card. This sort of villainy is not possible with smart cards because they store their information on a microchip that always encrypts information.

It is likely that, in the future, smart cards will use a combination of the following security systems to ensure the user of a card is who they say they are. You are likely to need to enter a secret code such as a PIN number. The card could also have a personalised token, like a photograph, embedded in it. Lastly, use of the system might also require some sort of bio-data such as iris or thumbprint recognition.

Multi-Function Smart Cards are capable of storing huge amounts of information. The following are just a few of the possible uses that they might be put to:

- Re-loadable tickets for public transport
- Medicare card
- Employer or student identification
- Drivers Licence
- Credit card
- Debit card (some organisations are calling this an 'e-purse'!)
- Business travel (payment for hotels, car rental, airlines, phone, travel agent, frequent flier points)
- Phone card
- Library card
- Building access
- Internet access & identification (authentication)
- Retail chain and entertainment discount cards

In the future we are likely to use smart cards instead of cash. We will be able to top up our smart cards with more e-cash via the Internet, at ATMs or by using a mobile phone. We are also likely to be able to trace the path of a transaction using the card.

Smart card readers will soon be incorporated into computers to enable us to make electronic commerce transactions. Security for purchasers on the Internet can be guaranteed by public key encryption. In this system you give your details and pay your money, not to a vendor, but to a bank on a branded Web page. When your details leave your card they are encrypted preventing the possibility of someone intercepting your card details. Lonely Planet, the travel guide company, has about 70 million visitors to its web-site every month. It has introduced a smart debit card system for services from its site including inexpensive long distance phone calls. Visitors to a site will also be able to download maps and holiday bookings. The site also offers free e-mail, a voice-mail facility and free Web voice mail.

> " Smart cards won't take off until a 'critical mass' of consumers start to use them for a wide variety of functions. Then the whole thing will explode. "

☐ Smart Card Acceptance by the Australian Public

Because of the widespread acceptance of e-commerce in Europe, only about half of all transactions there are with cash compared with 90% in most of the world. According to the Reserve Bank of Australia, seventeen percent of non-cash payments in Australia are made using credit cards, 22% by EFTPOS, 25% by direct entry debit and credit and 36% by cheque. Cheques are considered to be 'old technology' and it is expected that they will diminish in popularity, replaced by smart cards.

There is, however, some resistance by the Australian public to the adoption of smart cards. Some feel that they represent an invasion of privacy. That was the reason the government proposal to introduce the Australia Card was rejected some years ago. Smart cards have also suffered from news of unsuccessful trials and the general public still has concerns about security. Eventually, smart cards will become acceptable because they will be seen to make life more convenient. However, it is expected that people will not carry just one card with all functions on it because of the risk of losing it. Instead, people will carry a small number of cards and much less cash.

> " The replacement of physical cash by smart card payments promises massive savings in time and money. The central banks would print fewer bank notes. Fewer armed trucks would be needed to carry them and bank tellers would spend less time counting them. "

☐ Smart Operators

Capital One Finance Corporation, in the United States, has an advanced computer-assisted call answering service. Stored on its computer, the company has a large amount of information about each of its customers. When the computer registers a phone call it identifies the caller and uses a smart system to predict the purpose of the call. The call is then directed to the most suitable company agent (of the 3000 agents answering calls) who, by the time s/he answers the call, has information, on screen, about the customer. The information includes a suggestion about what the client might be interested in purchasing. After dealing with the client's reason for calling, the agent will determine if the client might like to make the purchase suggested by the computer. To head off callers who merely want a current balance, the first thing all callers will hear when the phone connects, is a computer voice giving them their current balance. This system has saved the company a lot of money and proved to be more efficient for customers.

❏ The Future

At the moment different smart cards have different standards. So some sort of global standard will need to be put in place. Pundits predict that the mass use of cards for public transport and telecommunications will be the key to widespread acceptance of smart cards. By 2003, it is expected that worldwide use of smart cards will be over 6 billion and smart transport cards will be used by 45 million Europeans. Twenty seven thousand Telstra smart pay phones now accept Telstra smart cards and Telstra is seen, by some, as the logical company to encourage the bank distribution of e-cash via pay phones instead of using ATMs.

INVENTIONS AND INNOVATIONS

☆ Main Point

The simultaneous maturing of so many different useful technologies has allowed inventors and innovators to exploit a vast array of promising synergies.

✓ Executive Summary

So much is happening so fast. Smarter, faster computers replace earlier models in months. Trends tend towards greater power and smaller size. New gadgets are being invented every day. With so many areas of interest to choose from, we had to be selective. We chose to look at some developments in the world of medicine, in personal transportation and computing. Genetics, lasers, microelectronics and virtual reality feature in the section on medicine. Links between video technology and computers feature in the section on cars. And computing is always changing with new ways to communicate and process information, new features for Internet sites and new ways to make life easier for people.

❖ The Big Ideas

1. Medicine

❐ Predicting Future Diseases

Over 4000 tests now exist for pre-disposition to certain diseases. Whether you are better off knowing about such things depends on the disease. If, for instance, your doctor is able to determine that you have a greater than normal chance of having a heart attack you can begin to take preventative measures with more exercise, a change of diet and drugs to reduce your susceptibility to heart attack. On the other hand there are diseases like Huntingdon's disease and Alzheimer's disease (brain diseases that affect thinking) that have no cure at the moment. Would you want to know about your pre-disposition to these diseases? Would you be able to cope with the knowledge? There are therefore ethical questions that doctors face when using tests to determine an individual's genetic pre-disposition to certain diseases.

❑ Probing the Brain

An analytical tool that may, one day, be useful in identifying early stage Alzheimer's disease is being trialled in the US. The tool, called Event Related Optical Signal (EROS) shoots low powered laser light into the brain to identify what parts of the brain deal with different functions such as language and memory and how the brain reacts to different stimuli.

❑ Spray-on Medication

Australian scientists have developed a means of administering drugs to patients that does not rely on the taking of pills or injections. Instead, a device looking something like an asthma inhaler is used to spray the medication onto the skin of the patient in a measured dose. The medication then goes straight into the bloodstream, bypassing the liver. The method would seem to be suitable for the treatment of many medical problems including Alzheimer's disease.

❑ Partial Sight for the Blind

People who have become blind through diseases of the retina may be able to have partial sight returned to them through the use of a silicon chip that can be attached to the retina. Light from outside will fall onto the silicon chip which will transmit electrical impulses to still active sites on the retina. These sites will then send impulses to the brain which will register light or dark. Scientists working in Australia, Germany and the US expect that patients will be able to recognise the difference between day and night, the shape of letters in large print text, the position of obstacles and the movement of objects. The images seen through these devices will be in the form of squares or dots of light and dark (pixilated vision).

❑ Virtual Training for Doctors

Training doctors to perform medical procedures has often meant their practicing on live patients. This can be traumatic to both the trainee and the patient. Now the Commonwealth Scientific and Industrial Research Organisation (CSIRO) has developed a virtual reality device that doctors can use for practice. The technique does not use a totally enclosed virtual reality environment, which would be exorbitantly expensive.

Instead doctors sit at a device that allows them to see (through special 3D glasses) their hands as they use an instrument (such as a scalpel or needle) to perform a procedure on the appropriate part of a patient. They hold a pen-like object that allows them to 'feel' scalpel on skin or bone. The view and feel experienced by the practicing doctor provides the illusion that they are performing a real procedure.

2. Smart Car Transportation

☐ Car PCs

Personal computers, specifically for cars, went on sale sometime last year. They are designed for the place in the dashboard reserved for the radio. They will respond to your verbal commands, for instance, to turn on your radio. They will also talk to you, giving road directions and read your e-mail to you. This year, the tire manufacturer, Goodyear, is set to release tires with a device that causes a dashboard light to flash if the pressure of the air in a tire becomes low.

☐ Intelligent Cruise Control and Beyond!

An intelligent cruise-control system is soon to be included in luxury cars like Mercedes-Benz, BMW and Audi. These devices essentially provide an extra pair of eyes on the road and hands on the wheel of the car, making decisions if the driver does not react in time. For instance, these systems ensure the car maintains a safe distance from other cars using a forward mounted radar sensor. If cars in front slow down, the car will automatically slow down and an alarm will sound. Other proposed functions include the use of a video camera on the road ahead to automatically keep the car in lane, recognise and stop at stop lights and brake if an obstacle appears. And no longer do you need to worry about someone stealing your smart car. If villains attempt to steal your car a new device, developed by Motorola, will not only cause the horn to beep and the headlights to flash but a message will be sent to your PC or mobile phone to alert you that an attempt has been made to steal your car. And when you get tired of your luxury land car, perhaps you will be ready to buy a Skycar. Late last year US tests were promised of a four passenger vehicle that takes off vertically and could travel up to 20 metres above the ground at an expected maximum speed of over 600km per hour.

3. Computing

☐ Improving Communication

Three devices that will soon be in the shops promise to revolutionise the way we communicate with each other. The first, developed by British Telecom, is called SmartQuill. It can be held like a pen and indeed, looks like a pen with a big bulb at the top. When the user writes, longhand, with it, the pen converts the words into digital form so that they can be entered into a word-processed document. The second invention, called E-fone, converts e-mail messages to the spoken word so that they can be easily accessed by phone. The third invention is electronic paper. This consists of a flexible plastic surface specially designed to accept and hold text or pictures (see High-Tech Entertainment). There are a number of attractive features about it. Firstly, it is re-usable. Just delete a down-loaded document and load up another one. It will be like a very light, portable computer monitor, complex enough to hold quite large documents. Because it is made of flexible plastic, the electronic paper can be wrapped around objects or even used for high resolution outdoor displays.

☐ Internet Enhancement

The Internet is great for finding information but it suffers the same fate as television in that it can only provide sound and two-dimensional images. Two inventions have been designed to enhance the Internet experience. Firstly, the people at digiscents.com are working on Smell-O-Vision! The company promises to add smell to sight and sound for your enjoyment. Although the technology is not yet ready for release, it is expected to involve the inclusion of a fragrance array reservoir in computer terminals. Combinations of the fragrances can then be electronically stimulated to communicate to the user a representation of a particular smell. The second invention, brought to you by the people at ipix.com, provides the user with an enhanced view of a scene. Click on what looks like an ordinary picture on the Internet and you can turn it through 360 degrees and up and down as if you were in the middle of the picture. The technique promises to be a useful aid for such people as real estate agents and those in the tourist industry and also in education.

☐ People-Centred Computing

US scientists have developed a device the size of a biscuit that can be worn in or on a piece of clothing that will communicate remotely with devices like home temperature and lighting controls, a remote personal alarm system and any other device that can function through remote sensing. They cost A$15. Another US company has designed a device that takes your body measurements so that a piece of clothing can be custom-made. The device consists of a small cubicle into which the customer steps. Six cameras around the cubicle take photographs of your body which are then analysed by a computer to describe your body shape and to specify the dimensions of a chosen garment.

Cameras have also been put to use in another device developed at the Australian National University. Called HAL Vision, the device can detect what you are looking at from your eye movements. Quadriplegics would be able to benefit from the device by directing the movement of a motorised wheelchair by eye movements alone.

☐ Computer Support

There is a trend in information technology and telecommunications towards the smaller and the more portable. For instance Motorola has recently announced the development of a new transistor (using materials called perovskites) that is smaller, thinner, faster and uses less energy than ever before. At the same time Bell Labs has announced the development of a transistor that is only 50-nanometres across. That is about 10 000 times smaller than the dot at the end of this sentence. Meanwhile, an Israeli firm has developed a low-cost battery that is about as thick as the dot at the end of this sentence. It can be used to power small devices and can be made any shape or size. Lastly, imagine that you are a geologists, exploring in the outback of Australia, hundreds of miles from everywhere and you need access to the company data base. A small, portable satellite 'dish' is now available that can allow the isolated explorer the luxury of using a laptop computer for video-conferencing and data transfer with home base.

Sailing Through Uncharted Waters in Inclement Weather

One of the best holidays we ever had was sailing the Whitsunday Islands with two other couples in a 40-foot yacht. One of the other couples were safety conscious and experienced sailors and we felt confident in their ability to 'captain' the vessel. As with all good sailors they checked maps and the weather frequently to keep us on course and away from potentially hazardous situations. They frequently checked the 'vital signs' in our environment and made decisions about what course to set to exploit vagaries of wind and tide. Sometimes they recognised the environment had changed and made adjustments to sails and direction. A major contribution to our successful trip was their expertise and attention to both details and 'the big picture' of our ever-changing environment.

Nowadays we all live, work and play at a time of unprecedented massive and fundamental change. This book has presented 'snapshots' of some of these changes in the worlds of business, technology and science. Key features of this time are the advent of the Internet, e-commerce and business-to-business transactions, the merging of telecommunications, Internet and entertainment functions and the continued impact of economic rationalism. Just as in sailing, in order for us to plan our lives we need to be aware of the nature of the changes around us and the ramifications they may have for our well-being.

However, with change comes uncertainty. We do not know what the future may hold. We try to keep up with the latest trends and make some reasonable predictions about the future. Then we have to make decisions and act. In times of great uncertainty we are bound to make mistakes. We choose to sell shares when we would have been better off to keep them and wait for a rebound. We choose to hire more staff only to find that we needed another mix, given subsequent events.

In such circumstances, our job is to recognise, as quickly as possible, when a mistake has been made and correct it before a disaster happens. It means scanning the environment all the time looking for changes and how they might affect our lives. In these uncertain times we must learn that decisions are made based on the known facts at the time. New facts may emerge or circumstances may change to make our original decision one that will lead us into trouble. So we need to be ready to reverse decisions and alter course in the light of new up-dated information. That is the best recipe for survival 'in uncharted waters and frequently inclement weather.'

So some of the most important rules of survival in these times might be summarised as follows:

- Keep a broad watching brief of the latest developments in all aspects of business, science and technology that could possibly influence the way you live, work and do business.

- Continue to identify features in this environment that might affect your life, work and business.

- When making decisions clearly identify what data and assumptions influenced the decision.

- Maintain a watching brief on this data and assumptions to determine their continued validity.

- Be prepared to change your mind in the light of new data.

- If you believe that you are intuitive, trust your intuition.

We trust this book will encourage you to continue to scan your environment for factors that may affect your future. If you are busy, like most of us, you don't have a lot of time to read all the newspapers and scan all the journals. So you need to select a few trusted sources of information and systematically use them to your advantage. We wish you good fortune in charting a course for your life, work and business in these uncertain times. And try a sailing holiday in the Whitsundays to reward yourself when you have some success!

Alan Cook & Heather Duggan

Brisbane, April 2000

How We Researched This Book

Frame Splicing

When I was very young my parents helped me plant some seeds in our garden. Every day I would go to the garden patch to see what was happening. Even when the seeds started to sprout I was disappointed that not very much happened from one day to the next. To help me see that changes were occurring, my father took photos of the plants every few days as they sprouted, grew and bloomed. Cinematographers use the same sort of technique to show the petals of a flower opening up. By splicing together single frames over time they can show the way the flower's petals open. They can demonstrate a trend.

We have borrowed this idea for the central research method used for this book. We realised that the reason it is so difficult to identify trends from the stories reported in the media is that the stories appear to us as a daily, dazzling mish-mash of isolated events. Reading the stories in newspapers or magazines on any one day only gives us accounts of different events that may or may not be single points in possible trends. At the start, at least, we can have no idea whether an event is part of an overall trend or not. To identify trends we need to look at a series of possibly related events over time.

Categorising

Over the second half of 1999 and early 2000 we searched newspapers, magazines, journals and the Internet on a daily basis. Each day we would snip out interesting articles and put them into categories that could possibly be related. There was a folder on life and living, another on government, another on science and one on commerce. As time went on, sub-categories emerged from within these categories and additional folders were started. New categories were identified and new folders filled. Apart from identifying categories, we made no concerted effort, at that stage, to identify trends.

Trendspotting

Late in 1999 we started to open folders to read the articles therein. In his book, Information Anxiety, Richard Saul

Wurman (1991) suggested that information could be ordered in only five different ways: by category, over time, by location, alphabetically and as part of a continuum. So, we began to sort the articles into piles that followed one of these ordered patterns. At the same time, trends tended to suggest themselves. For instance, more and more companies seemed to be seeking mergers, alliances or were part of takeovers. A range of separate developments were occurring in the field of genetics. It was clear that educators were having to become business people at the same time that businesses discovered there was money to be made from education via the Internet.

Checking & Predictions

While we began to describe some of these trends in short essays we continued to sample the media on a daily basis. This enabled us to gather additional information that either supported emerging trends or, in some cases, altered our thinking. In each essay we report what seemed to be happening and what commentators predicted would happen next. In some cases we added our own short-term predictions. Anybody who follows the stock market knows that seemingly unrelated events can conspire to change the course of history in the most unexpected of ways. Since we live in a time of massive change where so much is happening on so many fronts, we believe that it is of little value to extrapolate more than a few years into the future. So most of the predictions found in this book refer to the next year or two. There are few predictions in this book that extend past the next five years.

Format of the Book

We suspect that individuals with different needs might read this book. There are those, in a bookstore, who will flip through it to see if it might be of interest. We hope that the Main Points at the start of each essay might capture enough of their interest for them to buy the book! Then there are busy people who want to understand the essence of some trends but are not interested in the detail. For these individuals we wrote an Executive Summary. Lastly, there will be readers who wish to delve deeper into a topic to read details of events or examples of trends. For them the section of 'Big Ideas' should be useful. Some topics are intrinsically more technical than others. Since jargon tends to be a barrier to understanding, we have attempted, wherever possible, to replace jargon with plain English. Lastly, a few relevant quotations, that seem to capture the essence of the topics, accompany most essays.

Reading this Book

This book is not necessarily meant to be read starting at page one and continuing to the final page. The categories, Science, Technology, Business, Government and Living are designed to stand alone. Even the essays in each category are designed to be read separately. Readers can choose to read essays in any order.

Alan Cook & Heather Duggan

Reference:

R.S.Wurman (1991). Information Anxiety. London, Pan Books.

Index

About the Authors

Heather Duggan and Alan Cook are a husband and wife writing team living and working in Brisbane, Australia.

Heather Duggan is director of Mountain Pty Ltd, a consulting and publishing company. Heather specialises in Human Resources and Change Management. She has held senior management roles in the telecommunications industry, the mining industry and was Divisional Manager, Human Resources and Strategic Management with Brisbane City Council. A Fellow of the Australian Institute of Company Directors and a Fellow of the Australian Institute of Management as well as a charter member of the Australian Human Resources Institute, she is frequently called on to speak at regional and national conferences. Her work has taken her to Canada, Poland and the South Pacific.

Dr Alan Cook is a senior lecturer in Science Education at Queensland University of Technology in Brisbane. He teaches subjects such as Science, Technology and Society and Science and Technology in the Community and Workplace. This book was initially written for those students until it was clear that many in the community at large also were interested in an overview of all the changes swirling around us at the present time. Alan's roles as a teacher, teacher educator, researcher and curriculum developer have seen him work in the United Kingdom, Canada, Fiji and Tonga. He has spoken at conferences in most of the capital cities in Australia and as far afield as Jerusalem.

Between them Heather and Alan have three offspring, Kirby, Jim and Kathleen and one grandchild, Nadja. This book is dedicated to them, their spouses, Iris and Fred and the bright future the world promises them.

Thanks

We would like to thank Charlie Scandrett at Merino Litho for his cheerful, good humoured advice in the production of this book. David Wrigley of Avid Desktop Design, a renaissance man of the high tech world, had the patience of Job as he coped with changes upon changes while this book took form. We would also like to thank our good friends, Sonya Trau of Microsoft and Dr. Matt Trau of the University of Queensland for their feedback and encouragement. Dr. Neil Flanagan, co-author and publisher of Just About Everything A Manager Needs to Know gave readily of his time and allowed us some wonderful insights into the world of publishing. Lastly, we would like to thank Annabel Hepworth, Dan Coyne, Fiona Buffini, Helen Meredith, John Edwards, Trevor Sykes, Daewoo Automotive Australia and Queensland Newspapers who, when asked for permission to quote, gave it freely.

CYBER GOLD RUSH! – Order Form

ORDERING OPTIONS

Telephone orders: 07 3358 2014 (For VISA, MasterCard and Bankcard)

Fax orders: 07 3358 5885

On Line Orders: hduggan@powerup.com.au

Postal Orders: Mountain Pty Ltd, PO Box 556, New Farm, Queensland, 4005.

DELIVERY DETAILS   (Please Print)

Name: _____

Organisation: _____

Address: _____

City: _____ State: _____ Post Code: _____

Telephone: (   ) _____

Email: _____

PAYMENT

Price per book:	$24.95
After 1st July 2000 add 10% GST per book	$ 2.50
Postage: Add $6.00 in Australia (Books for Brisbane CBD will be delivered free of charge)	$

Number of books requested _____   Total Cost: _____

☐ Cheque: Made payable to Mountain Pty LTD

☐ VISA   ☐ Mastercard   ☐ Bankcard

Card Number: ☐☐☐☐ ☐☐☐☐ ☐☐☐☐ ☐☐☐☐

Name on card: _____ Exp. Date: ___ / ___ / ____

Signature: _____

Mountain Pty Ltd   PO Box 556 New Farm   Queensland Australia 4005
☎ 61 7 3358 2014   Fax: 61 7 3358 5885   Mobile: 0418 668 682